I0754903

THE ORDER
OF
CELEBRATING MATRIMONY

THE ROMAN RITUAL

RENEWED BY DECREE OF
THE MOST HOLY SECOND ECUMENICAL COUNCIL OF THE VATICAN,
PROMULGATED BY AUTHORITY OF POPE PAUL VI
AND REVISED AT THE DIRECTION OF POPE JOHN PAUL II

THE ORDER OF CELEBRATING MATRIMONY

ENGLISH TRANSLATION ACCORDING
TO THE SECOND TYPICAL EDITION

For Use in the Dioceses of the United States of America

Approved by the
United States Conference of Catholic Bishops
and Confirmed by the Apostolic See

CATHOLIC BOOK PUBLISHING CORP.
NEW JERSEY

2016

Concordat cum originali:
✠ Arthur J. Serratelli
Chairman, USCCB Committee on Divine Worship
after review by Reverend Michael J. Flynn
Executive Director, USCCB Secretariat of Divine Worship

Published by the authority of the Committee on Divine Worship,
United States Conference of Catholic Bishops

Latin text © Administration of the Patrimony of the Apostolic See (A.P.S.A.), Vatican City State, 1991.

Excerpts from the *Lectionary for Mass for Use in the Dioceses of the United States, second edition* Copyright © 1970, 1986, 1992, 1998, 2001 Confraternity of Christian Doctrine, Inc., Washington, D.C. All rights reserved. No part of this work may be reproduced or transmitted in any form or by any means, electronic or mechanical, including photocopying, recording, or by any information storage and retrieval system, without permission in writing from the copyright owner.

The Revised Grail Psalms Copyright © 2010, Conception Abbey/The Grail, admin. by GIA Publications, Inc., www.giamusic.com All rights reserved.

The English translation of Psalm Responses, Alleluia Verses, Gospel Verses from *Lectionary for Mass* © 1969, 1981, 1997, International Commission on English in the Liturgy Corporation (ICEL); excerpts from the English translation of *The Roman Missal* © 2010, ICEL; the English translation and chants of *The Order of Celebrating Matrimony* © 2013, ICEL. All rights reserved.

Latin Typical Edition, 1969.
Second Latin Typical Edition, 1991.
Reprint, 2008.

Some additional texts © 2016, United States Conference of Catholic Bishops, Washington, DC. All rights reserved. No part of this work may be reproduced or transmitted in any form or by any means, electronic or mechanical, including photocopying, recording, or by any information storage and retrieval system, without permission in writing from the copyright holder.

T-238

ISBN 978-1-941243-54-1 (238/22)

ISBN 978-1-941243-55-8 (238/13)

Illustrations and arrangement © 2016, Catholic Book Publishing Corp., N.J.

Printed in Korea

www.catholicbookpublishing.com

TABLE OF CONTENTS

CONGREGATION FOR DIVINE WORSHIP
AND THE DISCIPLINE OF THE SACRAMENTS

Prot. n. CD 1068/89

DECREE

The rite of celebrating Matrimony formerly found in the *Rituale Romanum* was reformed in accord with the decree of the Second Vatican Council by the promulgation in 1969 by the Sacred Congregation of Rites of the *Ordo celebrandi Matrimonium.*

In this second typical edition the same *Ordo* is presented with an enrichment of the Introduction, rites and prayers, and with certain changes introduced in keeping with the norm of the Code of Canon Law promulgated in 1983.

By special mandate of the Supreme Pontiff JOHN PAUL II, the Congregation for Divine Worship and the Discipline of the Sacraments publishes this new edition of the same *Ordo*. The *Ordo* in its second typical edition, composed in Latin, will come into force immediately upon publication; in vernacular languages, however, when translations have been confirmed by the Apostolic See, on the date decreed by Conferences of Bishops.

All things to the contrary notwithstanding.

From the offices of the Congregation for Divine Worship and the Discipline of the Sacraments, March 19, 1990, the Solemnity of Saint Joseph.

EDUARDO Cardinal MARTINEZ
Prefect

✠ Lajos Kada
Titular Archbishop of Tibica
Secretary

SACRED CONGREGATION OF RITES

Prot. n. R 23/969

DECREE

The *Ordo celebrandi Matrimonium*, revised in keeping with the norm of the decrees of the Constitution on the Sacred Liturgy, in order that it might be enriched, might signify more clearly the grace of the Sacrament, and might impart a knowledge of the obligations of the married couple, has been prepared by the Consilium for the Implementation of the Constitution on the Sacred Liturgy. Moreover, by his apostolic authority, the Supreme Pontiff PAUL VI, has approved this rite and ordered its publication. Therefore this Sacred Congregation of Rites, by special mandate of the Supreme Pontiff, promulgates it, directing that it be used from July 1, 1969.

All things to the contrary notwithstanding.

From the offices of the Sacred Congregation of Rites, March 19, 1969, the Solemnity of Saint Joseph, Spouse of the Blessed Virgin Mary.

BENNO Cardinal GUT
Prefect, Sacred Congregation of Rites
and President of the Consilium

✠ Ferdinand Antonelli
Titular Archbishop of Idicra
Secretary

CONGREGATION FOR DIVINE WORSHIP AND THE DISCIPLINE OF THE SACRAMENTS

Prot. n. 84/14

UNITED STATES OF AMERICA

At the request of His Excellency the Most Reverend Joseph E. Kurtz, Archbishop of Louisville, President of the Conference of Bishops of the United States of America, in a letter dated June 23, 2015, and by virtue of the faculty granted to this Congregation by the Supreme Pontiff FRANCIS, we gladly approve and confirm the text of the English-language translation of the *Ordo celebrandi Matrimonium, editio typica altera,* as found in the attached copy.

In printed editions, mention must be made of the approval and confirmation which this Congregation has conceded. Moreover, two copies of the printed text should be forwarded to this Congregation.

All things to the contrary notwithstanding.

From the offices of the Congregation for Divine Worship and the Discipline of the Sacraments, June 29, 2015, the Solemnity of Saints Peter and Paul, Apostles.

ROBERT Cardinal SARAH
Prefect

✠ ARTHUR ROCHE
Archbishop Secretary

UNITED STATES CONFERENCE OF CATHOLIC BISHOPS

DECREE OF PUBLICATION

In accord with the norms established by decree of the Sacred Congregation of Rites in *Cum, nostra œtate* (January 27, 1966) and of the Congregation for Divine Worship and the Discipline of the Sacraments in *Liturgiam authenticam* (March 28, 2001), this edition of the *Order of Celebrating Matrimony* is declared to be the vernacular typical edition of the *Ordo celebrandi Matrimonium, editio typica altera*, and is published by authority of the United States Conference of Catholic Bishops.

The *Order of Celebrating Matrimony* was canonically approved for use by the United States Conference of Catholic Bishops on November 12, 2013, and was subsequently confirmed by the Apostolic See by decree of the Congregation for Divine Worship and the Discipline of the Sacraments on June 29, 2015 (Prot. n. 84/14).

The *Order of Celebrating Matrimony* may be used in the Liturgy as of September 8, 2016, the Feast of the Nativity of the Blessed Virgin Mary, and its use is obligatory as of December 30, 2016, the Feast of the Holy Family of Jesus, Mary and Joseph. From that date forward, no other English edition of the *Order of Celebrating Matrimony* may be used in the dioceses of the United States of America.

Given at the General Secretariat of the United States Conference of Catholic Bishops, Washington, DC, on February 2, 2016, the Feast of the Presentation of the Lord.

✠ JOSEPH E. KURTZ
Archbishop of Louisville
President, United States Conference of Catholic Bishops

Reverend Monsignor J. BRIAN BRANSFIELD
General Secretary

INTRODUCTION

I. The Importance and Dignity of the Sacrament of Matrimony

1. The matrimonial covenant, by which a man and a woman establish a lifelong partnership between themselves,[1] derives its force and strength from creation, but for the Christian faithful it is also raised up to a higher dignity, since it is numbered among the Sacraments of the new covenant.

2. A Marriage is established by the conjugal covenant, that is, the irrevocable consent of both spouses, by which they freely give themselves to each other and accept each other. Moreover, this singular union of a man and a woman requires, and the good of the children demands, the complete fidelity of the spouses and the indissoluble unity of the bond.[2]

3. Furthermore, the institution of Marriage itself and conjugal love are, by their very nature, ordered to the procreation and formation of children and find in them, as it were, their ultimate crown.[3] Children are thus truly the supreme gift of Marriage and contribute greatly to the good of the parents themselves.

4. The intimate community of life and love, by which spouses "are no longer two, but one flesh,"[4] has been established by God the Creator, provided with its own proper laws, and endowed with that blessing which alone was not forfeited by punishment for original sin.[5] This sacred bond, therefore, does not depend on human choice, but rather on the Author of Marriage, who ordained it to be endowed with its own goods and ends.[6]

5. Indeed Christ the Lord, making a new creation and making all things new,[7] has willed that Marriage be restored to its primordial form and holiness in such a way that what God has joined together, no one may put asunder,[8] and raised this indissoluble conjugal contract to the dignity of a Sacrament so that it might signify more clearly and represent more easily the model of his own nuptial covenant with the Church.[9]

---

[1] Cf. *Codex Iuris Canonici* (C.I.C.) can. 1055, §1.

[2] Cf. Second Vatican Council, Pastoral Constitution on the Church in the Modern World, *Gaudium et spes*, no. 48.

[3] Cf. *ibid.*

[4] Matthew 19:6.

[5] Cf. Nuptial Blessing.

[6] Cf. Second Vatican Council, Pastoral Constitution on the Church in the Modern World, *Gaudium et spes*, no. 48.

[7] Cf. 2 Corinthians 5:17.

[8] Cf. Matthew 19:6.

[9] Cf. Second Vatican Council, Pastoral Constitution on the Church in the Modern World, *Gaudium et spes*, no. 48.

6. By his presence, Christ brought blessing and joy to the wedding at Cana, where he changed water into wine and so foreshadowed the hour of the new and eternal covenant: "For just as of old God made himself present to his people with a covenant of love and fidelity, so now the Savior of the human race"[10] offers himself to the Church as Spouse, fulfilling his covenant with her in his Paschal Mystery.

7. Through Baptism, which is the Sacrament of faith, a man and a woman are once and for all incorporated into the covenant of Christ with the Church in such a way that their conjugal community is assumed into Christ's charity and is enriched by the power of his Sacrifice.[11] From this new condition it follows that a valid Marriage between the baptized is always a Sacrament.[12]

8. By the Sacrament of Matrimony Christian spouses signify and participate in the mystery of unity and fruitful love between Christ and the Church;[13] therefore, both in embracing conjugal life and in accepting and educating their children, they help one another to become holy and have their own place and particular gift among the People of God.[14]

9. Through this Sacrament the Holy Spirit brings it about that, just as Christ loved the Church and gave himself up for her,[15] Christian spouses also strive to nurture and foster their union in equal dignity, mutual giving, and the undivided love that flows from the divine font of charity. In this way, uniting divine and human realities, they persevere in good times and in bad, faithful in body and mind,[16] remaining complete strangers to any adultery and divorce.[17]

10. The true development of conjugal love and the whole meaning of family life, without diminishment of the other ends of Marriage, are directed to disposing Christian spouses to cooperate wholeheartedly with the love of the Creator and Savior, who through them increases and enriches his family from day to day.[18] Therefore, trusting in divine Providence and developing a spirit of sacrifice,[19] they glorify the Creator and strive for perfection in Christ, as they carry out the role of procreation with generous, human and Christian responsibility.[20]

---

[10] *Ibid.*

[11] Cf. John Paul II, Apostolic Exhortation, *Familiaris consortio*, no. 13: *Acta Apostolicae Sedis* (*A.A.S.*) 74 (1982), 95; cf. Second Vatican Council, Pastoral Constitution on the Church in the Modern World, *Gaudium et spes*, no. 48.

[12] Cf. C.I.C., can. 1055, §2.

[13] Cf. Ephesians 5:25.

[14] Cf. 1 Corinthians 7:7; Second Vatican Council, Dogmatic Constitution on the Church, *Lumen gentium*, no. 11.

[15] Cf. Ephesians 5:25.

[16] Cf. Second Vatican Council, Pastoral Constitution on the Church in the Modern World, *Gaudium et spes*, nos. 48, 50.

[17] Cf. *ibid.*, no. 49.

[18] Cf. *ibid.*, no. 50.

[19] Cf. 1 Corinthians 7:5.

[20] Cf. Second Vatican Council, Pastoral Constitution on the Church in the Modern World, *Gaudium et spes*, no. 50.

11. For God, who has called the couple to Marriage, continues to call them to Marriage.[21] Those who marry in Christ are able, with faith in the Word of God, to celebrate fruitfully the mystery of the union of Christ and the Church, to live it rightly, and to bear witness to it publicly before all. A Marriage that is desired, prepared for, celebrated, and lived daily in the light of faith is that which is "joined by the Church, strengthened by a sacrificial offering, sealed by a blessing, announced by Angels, and ratified by the Father. . . . How wonderful the bond of the two believers: one in hope, one in vow, one in discipline, one in the same service! They are both children of one Father and servants of the same Master, with no separation of spirit and flesh. Indeed, they are two in one flesh; where there is one flesh, there is also one spirit."[22]

II. Duties and Ministries

12. The preparation and celebration of Marriage, which above all concern the future spouses themselves and their families, belong, as regards pastoral and liturgical care, to the Bishop, to the pastor and his associates, and, at least to some degree, to the entire ecclesial community.[23]

13. It is for the Bishop, who is to take into account any norms or pastoral guidelines that may have been established by the Conference of Bishops regarding the preparation of engaged couples or the pastoral care of Marriage, to regulate the celebration and pastoral care of the Sacrament throughout the diocese by organizing assistance for the Christian faithful so that the state of Marriage may be preserved in a Christian spirit and advance in perfection.[24]

14. Pastors of souls must take care that in their own community this assistance is provided especially:

1) by preaching, by catechesis adapted to children, young people, and adults, and through means of social communication, so that the Christian faithful are instructed about the meaning of Christian Marriage and about the role of Christian spouses and parents;

2) by personal preparation for entering Marriage, so that those to be married are disposed to the holiness and duties of their new state;

3) by a fruitful liturgical celebration of Marriage, so that it becomes clear that the spouses signify and participate in the mystery of the unity and fruitful love between Christ and the Church;

---

[21] Cf. John Paul II, Apostolic Exhortation, *Familiaris consortio*, no. 51: *A.A.S.* 74 (1982), 143.

[22] Tertullian, *Ad uxorem*, II, VIII: *CCL* I, 393.

[23] Cf. John Paul II, Apostolic Exhortation, *Familiaris consortio*, no. 66: *A.A.S.* 74 (1982), 159-162.

[24] Cf. *ibid.*; cf. C.I.C., can. 1063-1064.

4) by help offered to those who are married, so that, faithfully preserving and protecting the conjugal covenant, they daily come to lead a holier and fuller family life.[25]

15. Sufficient time is required for a suitable preparation for Marriage. Engaged couples should be made aware of this necessity in advance.

16. Led by the love of Christ, pastors are to welcome engaged couples and, above all, to foster and nourish their faith: for the Sacrament of Matrimony presupposes and demands faith.[26]

17. The engaged couple, having been reminded, if appropriate, of the fundamental elements of Christian doctrine mentioned above (nos. 1-11) should be given catechesis not only about the Church's teaching on Marriage and the family but also about the Sacrament and its rites, prayers, and readings, so that they may be able to celebrate it thoughtfully and fruitfully.

18. Catholics who have not yet received the Sacrament of Confirmation are to receive it to complete their Christian Initiation before they are admitted to Marriage if this can be done without grave inconvenience. It is recommended to the engaged couple that in preparation for the Sacrament of Matrimony they receive the Sacrament of Penance, if necessary, and that they approach the Most Holy Eucharist, especially within the celebration of Marriage itself.[27]

19. Before a Marriage is celebrated, it must be established that nothing stands in the way of its valid and licit celebration.[28]

20. In conducting the preparation, pastors, taking into account prevailing attitudes toward Marriage and the family, should endeavor to evangelize the couple's authentic and mutual love in the light of faith. Even the requirements of law for contracting a valid and licit Marriage can serve to promote a living faith and fruitful love between the couple, ordered toward establishing a Christian family.

21. But if every effort fails, and an engaged couple openly and expressly demonstrate that they reject what the Church intends when the Marriage of baptized persons is celebrated, the pastor of souls is not permitted to celebrate the Sacrament. Though reluctant, he must take note of the situation and convince those involved that, in these circumstances, it is not the Church, but they themselves, who prevent the celebration they are asking for.[29]

---

[25]Cf. C.I.C., can. 1063.

[26]Cf. Second Vatican Council, Constitution on the Sacred Liturgy, *Sacrosanctum Concilium*, no. 59.

[27]Cf. C.I.C., can. 1065.

[28]Cf. *ibid.*, can. 1066.

[29]Cf. John Paul II, Apostolic Exhortation, *Familiaris consortio*, no. 68: *A.A.S.* 74 (1982), 165.

22. With regard to Marriage, it is by no means rare for special cases to arise: such as Marriage with a baptized non-Catholic, with a catechumen, with a person who is simply unbaptized, or even with a person who has explicitly rejected the Catholic faith. Those in charge of pastoral care should keep in mind the norms of the Church pertaining to these types of cases, and they should, if the occasion requires, have recourse to the competent authority.

23. It is appropriate that the same Priest who prepares the engaged couple should, during the celebration of the Sacrament itself, give the Homily, receive the spouses' consent, and celebrate the Mass.

24. It also pertains to a Deacon, after receiving the faculty from the pastor or from the local Ordinary, to preside at the celebration of the Sacrament,[30] without omitting the Nuptial Blessing.

25. Where there is a shortage of Priests and Deacons, the Diocesan Bishop can delegate laypersons to assist at Marriages, after a prior favorable vote of the Conference of Bishops and after the permission of the Apostolic See has been obtained. A suitable layperson is to be selected, who is capable of giving instruction to those preparing to be married and able to perform the Marriage liturgy properly.[31] The layperson asks for the consent of the spouses and receives it in the name of the Church.[32]

26. Other laypersons, however, can play a part in various ways both in the spiritual preparation of the engaged couple and in the celebration of the rite itself. Moreover, the entire Christian community should cooperate to bear witness to the faith and to be a sign to the world of Christ's love.

27. The Marriage is to be celebrated in the parish of one or other of the engaged persons, or elsewhere with the permission of the proper Ordinary or pastor.[33]

III. The Celebration of Matrimony

The Preparation

28. Since Marriage is ordered toward the increase and sanctification of the People of God, its celebration displays a communitarian character that encourages the participation also of the parish community, at least through some of its members. With due regard for local customs and as occasion suggests, several Marriages may be celebrated at the same time or the celebration of the Sacrament may take place during the Sunday assembly.

[30] Cf. C.I.C., can. 1111.

[31] Cf. *ibid.*, can. 1112, §2.

[32] Cf. *ibid.*, can. 1108, §2.

[33] Cf. *ibid.*, can. 1115.

29. The celebration itself of the Sacrament must be diligently prepared, as far as possible, with the engaged couple. Marriage should normally be celebrated within Mass. Nevertheless, with due regard both for the necessities of pastoral care and for the way in which the prospective spouses and those present participate in the life of the Church, the pastor should decide whether it would be preferable to propose that Marriage be celebrated within or outside of Mass.[34] The following should be chosen with the engaged couple, as the circumstances so suggest: the readings from Sacred Scripture, which will be explained in the Homily; the form for expressing mutual consent; the formularies for the blessing of rings, for the Nuptial Blessing, for the intentions of the Universal Prayer or Prayer of the Faithful, and for the chants. Moreover, attention should also be given to the appropriate use of options provided in the rite as well as to local customs, which may be observed if appropriate.

30. The chants to be sung during the Rite of Marriage should be appropriate and should express the faith of the Church, with attention paid to the importance of the Responsorial Psalm within the Liturgy of the Word. What is said concerning the chants applies also to the selection of other musical works.

31. The festive character of the celebration of Marriage should be suitably expressed even in the manner of decorating the church. Nevertheless, local Ordinaries are to be vigilant that, apart from the honors due to civil authorities in keeping with the norm of liturgical laws, no favoritism be shown to private persons or classes of persons.[35]

32. If a Marriage is celebrated on a day having a penitential character, especially during Lent, the pastor is to counsel the spouses to take into account the special nature of that day. The celebration of Marriage on Friday of the Passion of the Lord and Holy Saturday is to be avoided altogether.

The Rite to Be Used

33. In the celebration of Marriage within Mass, the rite described in Chapter I is used. In the celebration of Marriage without Mass, the rite should take place after a Liturgy of the Word according to the norm of Chapter II.

34. Whenever Marriage is celebrated within Mass, the Ritual Mass "The Celebration of Marriage" is used with sacred vestments of the color white or of a festive color. On those days listed in nos. 1-4 of the Table of Liturgical Days, however, the Mass of the day is used with its own readings, with inclusion of the Nuptial Blessing and, if appropriate, the proper formula for the final blessing.

---

[34] Cf. Second Vatican Council, Constitution on the Sacred Liturgy, *Sacrosanctum Concilium*, no. 78.
[35] Cf. *ibid.*, no. 32.

If, however, during Christmas and Ordinary Time, the parish community participates in a Sunday Mass during which Marriage is celebrated, the Mass of the Sunday is used.

Nevertheless, since a Liturgy of the Word adapted for the celebration of Marriage has a great impact in the handing on of catechesis about the Sacrament itself and about the duties of the spouses, when the Mass "For the Celebration of Marriage" is not said, one of the readings may be taken from the texts provided for the celebration of Marriage (nos. 144-187).

35. The main elements of the celebration of Marriage are to stand out clearly, namely: the Liturgy of the Word, in which are expressed the importance of Christian Marriage in the history of salvation and the responsibilities and duties of Marriage to be attended to for the sanctification of the spouses and of their children; the consent of the contracting parties, which the person assisting asks for and receives; the venerable prayer by which the blessing of God is invoked upon the bride and bridegroom; finally, Eucharistic Communion of both spouses and of others present, by which, above all, their charity is nurtured and they are raised up to communion with the Lord and with their neighbor.[36]

36. If a Marriage takes place between a Catholic and a baptized non-Catholic, the rite for celebrating Matrimony without Mass (nos. 79-117) should be used. If, however, the situation warrants it, the rite for celebrating Matrimony within Mass (nos. 45-78) may be used, with the consent of the local Ordinary; but with regard to admission of the non-Catholic party to Eucharistic Communion, the norms issued for various cases are to be observed.[37] If a Marriage takes place between a Catholic and a catechumen or a non-Christian, the rite given below (nos. 118-143) is to be used, with the variations provided for different situations.

37. Although pastors are ministers of Christ's Gospel for all, they should, nonetheless, direct special attention to those, whether Catholics or non-Catholics, who never or rarely take part in the celebration of Marriage or the Eucharist. This pastoral norm applies in the first place to the spouses themselves.

38. If Marriage is celebrated within Mass, in addition to those things required for the celebration of Mass, *The Order of Celebrating Matrimony* and rings for the spouses should be prepared in the sanctuary. There should also be prepared, if appropriate, a vessel of holy water with an aspergillum and a chalice of sufficient size for Communion under both kinds.

[36]Cf. Second Vatican Council, Decree on the Apostolate of the Laity, *Apostolicam actuositatem*, no. 3; Dogmatic Constitution on the Church, *Lumen gentium*, no. 12.

[37]Cf. C.I.C., can. 844.

IV. Adaptations to Be Prepared by the Conferences of Bishops

39. It is for the Conferences of Bishops, by virtue of the Constitution on the Sacred Liturgy,[38] to adapt this Roman Ritual to the customs and needs of the particular regions, so that, once their decisions have been accorded the *recognitio* of the Apostolic See, the edition may be used in the regions to which it pertains.

40. In this regard, it is for the Conferences of Bishops:

1) To formulate the adaptations indicated below (nos. 41-44).

2) If necessary, to adapt and supplement this Introduction of the Roman Ritual from no. 36 and what follows (in "The Rite to Be Used"), so as to achieve the conscious and active participation of the faithful.

3) To prepare versions of the texts, so that they are truly accommodated to the nature of different languages and the character of diverse cultures, and to add, whenever appropriate, suitable melodies for singing.

4) In preparing editions, to arrange the material in a form more suitable for pastoral use.

41. In preparing adaptations, the following points should be kept in mind:

1) The formulas of the Roman Ritual may be adapted and, if necessary, even supplemented (even the questions before the consent and the words of the consent themselves).

2) Whenever the Roman Ritual gives several optional formulas, it is permitted to add other formulas of the same kind.

3) Provided the structure of the sacramental rite is preserved, the order of the parts may be adapted. If it seems more appropriate, the questions before the consent may be omitted, provided the law is observed that the person assisting ask for and receive the consent of the contracting parties.

4) Should pastoral need so demand, it can be determined that the consent of the contracting parties always be sought by questioning.

5) After the giving of rings, in keeping with local customs, the crowning of the bride or the veiling of the spouses may take place.

6) Wherever the joining of hands or the blessing and giving of rings are incompatible with the culture of the people, it may be decided that these rites be omitted or replaced by other rites.

7) It should be carefully and prudently considered what elements from the traditions and culture of particular peoples may appropriately be adopted.

[38]Cf. Second Vatican Council, Constitution on the Sacred Liturgy, *Sacrosanctum Concilium*, nos. 37-40 and 63b.

42. In addition, in accordance with the norm of the Constitution on the Sacred Liturgy (no. 63b), each Conference of Bishops has the faculty to draw up its own Marriage rite appropriate to the customs of the place and the people, with the decision approved by the Apostolic See, provided the law is observed that the person assisting must ask for and receive the consent of the contracting parties[39] and the Nuptial Blessing must be given.[40] The Introduction in the Roman Ritual is to be prefixed even to a proper ritual,[41] except for those points that refer to the rite to be used.

43. In the usages and ways of celebrating Marriage prevailing among peoples now receiving the Gospel for the first time, whatever is honorable and not indissolubly connected with superstition and errors should be sympathetically considered and, if possible, preserved intact, and in fact even admitted into the Liturgy itself as long as it harmonizes with a true and authentic liturgical spirit.[42]

44. Among peoples for whom the Marriage ceremonies customarily take place in homes, even over a period of several days, these ceremonies should be adapted to the Christian spirit and to the Liturgy. In this case the Conference of Bishops, in accordance with the pastoral needs of the people, may determine that the rite of the Sacrament itself can be celebrated in homes.

[39] Cf. Second Vatican Council, Constitution on the Sacred Liturgy, *Sacrosanctum Concilium*, no. 77.

[40] Cf. *ibid.*, no. 78.

[41] Cf. *ibid.*, no. 63b.

[42] Cf. *ibid.*, no. 37.

RAPHAEL·VRBINAS
M
DIIII

CHAPTER I

THE ORDER OF CELEBRATING MATRIMONY WITHIN MASS

THE INTRODUCTORY RITES

The First Form

45. At the appointed time, the Priest, wearing an alb and a stole and chasuble of the color of the Mass to be celebrated, goes with the servers to the door of the church, receives the bridal party, and warmly greets them, showing that the Church shares in their joy.

46. The procession to the altar then takes place in the customary manner. Meanwhile, the Entrance Chant takes place.

47. The Priest approaches the altar, reverences it with a profound bow, and venerates it with a kiss. After this, he goes to the chair.

The Second Form

48. At the appointed time, the Priest, wearing an alb and a stole and chasuble of the color of the Mass to be celebrated, goes with the servers to the place prepared for the couple or to his chair.

49. When the couple have arrived at their place, the Priest receives them and warmly greets them, showing that the Church shares in their joy.

50. Then, during the Entrance Chant, the Priest approaches the altar, reverences it with a profound bow, and venerates it with a kiss. After this, he goes to the chair.

---

51. Then, after the Sign of the Cross has been made, the Priest greets those present, using one of the formulas provided in *The Roman Missal.*

52. Then, in these or similar words, the Priest addresses the couple and those present to dispose them inwardly for the celebration of Marriage:

We have come rejoicing into the house of the Lord
for this celebration, dear brothers and sisters,
and now we stand with N. and N.
on the day they intend to form a home of their own.
For them this is a moment of unique importance.
So let us support them
with our affection,
with our friendship,
and with our prayer as their brothers and sisters.
Let us listen attentively with them
to the word that God speaks to us today.
Then, with holy Church,
let us humbly pray to God the Father,
through Christ our Lord,
for this couple, his servants,
that he lovingly accept them,
bless them,
and make them always one.

53. Or:

N. and N., the Church shares your joy
and warmly welcomes you,
together with your families and friends,
as today,
in the presence of God our Father,
you establish between yourselves
a lifelong partnership.
May the Lord hear you on this your joyful day.
May he send you help from heaven and protect you.
May he grant you your hearts' desire
and fulfill every one of your prayers.

The Penitential Act is omitted. The Gloria in excelsis (Glory to God in the highest) is said according to the rubric of the Roman Missal, Ritual Masses, V. For the Celebration of Marriage.

54. On those days when Ritual Masses are permitted, the Mass "For the Celebration of Marriage" is used with the proper readings.

However, on those days listed in nos. 1-4 of the Table of Liturgical Days, the Mass of the day is used, retaining the Nuptial Blessing in the Mass and, if appropriate, the proper formula for the final blessing.

If, however, during Christmas and Ordinary Time, the parish community participates in a Sunday Mass during which Marriage is celebrated, the Mass of the Sunday is used.

THE LITURGY OF THE WORD

55. The Liturgy of the Word is celebrated in the usual manner. There may be three readings, of which the First Reading should be from the Old Testament, but, during Easter Time, from the Book of Revelation (nos. 144-187). At least one reading that explicitly speaks of Marriage must always be chosen.

56. When the Ritual Mass is not said, one of the readings may be taken from those provided in the Lectionary for that Mass, except on a day listed in nos. 1-4 of the Table of Liturgical Days.

Readings that particularly express the importance and dignity of Marriage in the mystery of salvation are provided here.

The First Reading

Genesis 1:26-28, 31a

A reading from the Book of Genesis

Male and female he created them.

Then God said:
"Let us make man in our image, after our likeness.
Let them have dominion over the fish of the sea,
the birds of the air, and the cattle,
and over all the wild animals
and all the creatures that crawl on the ground."

God created man in his image;
in the image of God he created him;
male and female he created them.

God blessed them, saying:
"Be fertile and multiply;
fill the earth and subdue it.
Have dominion over the fish of the sea, the birds of the air,
and all the living things that move on the earth."
God looked at everything he had made, and he found it very good.

The word of the Lord.

Responsorial Psalm

Psalm 128:1-2, 3, 4-5ac and 6a

℟. (see 1a) Blessed are those who fear the Lord.

or:

℟. (4) See how the Lord blesses those who fear him.

Blessed are all who fear the Lord,
and walk in his ways!
By the labor of your hands you shall eat.
You will be blessed and prosper.

℟. Blessed are those who fear the Lord.

or:

℟. See how the Lord blesses those who fear him.

Your wife like a fruitful vine
in the heart of your house;
your children like shoots of the olive
around your table.

℟. Blessed are those who fear the Lord.

or:

℟. See how the Lord blesses those who fear him.

Indeed thus shall be blessed
the man who fears the Lord.
May the Lord bless you from Zion
all the days of your life!
May you see your children's children.

℟. Blessed are those who fear the Lord.

or:

℟. See how the Lord blesses those who fear him.

The Second Reading

Ephesians 5:2a, 25-32

A reading from the Letter of Saint Paul to the Ephesians

This is a great mystery, but I speak in reference to Christ and the Church.

Brothers and sisters:
Live in love, as Christ loved us
and handed himself over for us.

Husbands, love your wives,
even as Christ loved the Church
and handed himself over for her to sanctify her,
cleansing her by the bath of water with the word,
that he might present to himself the Church in splendor,
without spot or wrinkle or any such thing,
that she might be holy and without blemish.
So also husbands should love their wives as their own bodies.
He who loves his wife loves himself.
For no one hates his own flesh
but rather nourishes and cherishes it,
even as Christ does the Church,
because we are members of his Body.

For this reason a man shall leave his father and his mother
and be joined to his wife,
and the two shall become one flesh.

This is a great mystery,
but I speak in reference to Christ and the Church.

The word of the Lord.

The Alleluia and the Verse before the Gospel

Psalm 134:3

℟. Alleluia, alleluia.

May the Lord bless you from Zion,
he who made both heaven and earth.

℟. Alleluia, alleluia.

Or, during Lent: cf. 1 John 4:16b, 12, 11

℟. (Psalm 81:2) Sing joyfully to God our strength.

God is love.
let us love one another, as God has loved us.

℟. Sing joyfully to God our strength.

The Gospel

Matthew 19:3-6

✠ **A reading from the holy Gospel according to Matthew**

What God has united, man must not separate.

Some Pharisees approached Jesus, and tested him, saying,
"Is it lawful for a man to divorce his wife for any cause whatever?"
He said in reply, "Have you not read that from the beginning
the Creator *made them male and female* and said,
For this reason a man shall leave his father and mother
and be joined to his wife, and the two shall become one flesh?
So they are no longer two, but one flesh.
Therefore, what God has joined together, man must not separate."

The Gospel of the Lord.

57. After the reading of the Gospel, the Priest in the Homily uses the sacred text to expound the mystery of Christian Marriage, the dignity of conjugal love, the grace of the Sacrament, and the responsibilities of married people, keeping in mind, however, the various circumstances of individuals.

THE CELEBRATION OF MATRIMONY

58. If two or more Marriages happen to be celebrated at the same time, the Questions before the Consent, the Consent itself, and also the Reception of the Consent must always take place individually for each Marriage; the remaining parts, however, including the Nuptial Blessing, should be spoken once for all in the plural.

59. With all standing, including the couple and the witnesses, who are positioned near them, the Priest addresses the couple in these or similar words:

Dearly beloved,
you have come together into the house of the Church,
so that in the presence of the Church's minister
and the community
your intention to enter into Marriage
may be strengthened by the Lord with a sacred seal.
Christ abundantly blesses the love that binds you.
Through a special Sacrament,
he enriches and strengthens
those he has already consecrated by Holy Baptism,
that they may be faithful to each other for ever
and assume all the responsibilities of married life.
And so, in the presence of the Church,
I ask you to state your intentions.

The Questions before the Consent

60. The Priest then questions them about their freedom of choice, fidelity to each other, and the acceptance and upbringing of children, and each responds separately.

**N. and N., have you come here to enter into Marriage without coercion,
freely and wholeheartedly?**

The bridegroom and bride each say:

I have.

The Priest continues:

**Are you prepared, as you follow the path of Marriage,
to love and honor each other
for as long as you both shall live?**

The bridegroom and bride each say:

I am.

The following question may be omitted, if circumstances suggest this, for example, if the couple are advanced in years.

**Are you prepared to accept children lovingly from God
and to bring them up
according to the law of Christ and his Church?**

The bridegroom and bride each say:

I am.

The Consent

61. The Priest invites them to declare their consent:

**Since it is your intention to enter the covenant
of Holy Matrimony,
join your right hands and declare your consent
before God and his Church.**

They join their right hands.

62. The bridegroom says:

I, N., take you, N., to be my wife.
I promise to be faithful to you,
in good times and in bad,
in sickness and in health,
to love you and to honor you
all the days of my life.

The bride says:

I, N., take you, N., to be my husband.
I promise to be faithful to you,
in good times and in bad,
in sickness and in health,
to love you and to honor you
all the days of my life.

The following alternative form may be used:

The bridegroom says:

I, N., take you, N., for my lawful wife,
to have and to hold, from this day forward,
for better, for worse,
for richer, for poorer,
in sickness and in health,
to love and to cherish
until death do us part.

The bride says:

I, N., take you, N., for my lawful husband,
to have and to hold, from this day forward,
for better, for worse,
for richer, for poorer,
in sickness and in health,
to love and to cherish
until death do us part.

---

63. If, however, it seems preferable for pastoral reasons, the Priest may obtain the consent of the contracting parties through questioning.

First, he asks the bridegroom:

**N., do you take N., to be your wife?
Do you promise to be faithful to her
in good times and in bad,
in sickness and in health,
to love her and to honor her
all the days of your life?**

The bridegroom replies:

I do.

Next, the Priest asks the bride:

**N., do you take N., to be your husband?
Do you promise to be faithful to him
in good times and in bad,
in sickness and in health,
to love him and to honor him
all the days of your life?**

The bride replies:

I do.

The following alternative form may be used:

First, he asks the bridegroom:

N., do you take N. for your lawful wife,
to have and to hold, from this day forward,
for better, for worse,
for richer, for poorer,
in sickness and in health,
to love and to cherish
until death do you part?

The bridegroom replies:

I do.

Next, the Priest asks the bride:

N., do you take N. for your lawful husband,
to have and to hold, from this day forward,
for better, for worse,
for richer, for poorer,
in sickness and in health,
to love and to cherish
until death do you part?

The bride replies:

I do.

The Reception of the Consent

64. Then, receiving their consent, the Priest says to the bride and bridegroom:

May the Lord in his kindness strengthen the consent
you have declared before the Church,
and graciously bring to fulfillment
his blessing within you.
What God joins together, let no one put asunder.

Or:

May the God of Abraham, the God of Isaac,
the God of Jacob,
the God who joined together our first parents in paradise,
strengthen and bless in Christ
the consent you have declared before the Church,
so that what God joins together, no one may put asunder.

65. The Priest invites those present to praise God:

Let us bless the Lord.

All reply:

Thanks be to God.

Another acclamation may be sung or said.

The Blessing and Giving of Rings

66. The Priest says:

May the Lord bless ✠ these rings,
which you will give to each other
as a sign of love and fidelity.

℟. Amen.

Other formulas for blessing the rings, nos. 194-195.

He sprinkles the rings, as the circumstances so suggest, and gives them to the bride and bridegroom.

67A. The husband places his wife's ring on her ring finger, saying, as the circumstances so suggest:

N., receive this ring
as a sign of my love and fidelity.
In the name of the Father, and of the Son,
and of the Holy Spirit.

Likewise, the wife places her husband's ring on his ring finger, saying, as the circumstances so suggest:

N., receive this ring
as a sign of my love and fidelity.
In the name of the Father, and of the Son,
and of the Holy Spirit.

THE BLESSING AND GIVING OF THE *ARRAS*

67B. If the occasion so suggests, the rite of blessing and giving of the *arras* (coins) may take place following the blessing and giving of rings.

The Priest says:

Bless, ✠ O Lord, these *arras*
that N. and N. will give to each other
and pour over them the abundance of
your good gifts.

The husband takes the *arras* and hands them over to his wife, saying:

N., receive these *arras* as a pledge of God's blessing
and a sign of the good gifts we will share.

The wife takes the *arras* and hands them over to the husband, saying:

N., receive these *arras* as a pledge of God's blessing
and a sign of the good gifts we will share.

68. Then a hymn or canticle of praise may be sung by the whole community.

THE UNIVERSAL PRAYER

69. The Universal Prayer then takes place in the usual manner (examples are provided in nos. 216-217).

After this, the Symbol or Creed is said, if required by the rubrics.

THE LITURGY OF THE EUCHARIST

70. If appropriate, at the Preparation of the Gifts the bride and bridegroom may bring the bread and wine to the altar.

71A. A commemoration of the husband and wife in the Eucharistic Prayer is made with a formula provided in nos. 202-204.

THE BLESSING AND PLACING OF THE *LAZO* OR THE VEIL

71B. According to local customs, the rite of blessing and imposition of the *lazo* (wedding garland) or of the veil may take place before the Nuptial Blessing. The spouses remain kneeling in their place. If the *lazo* has not been placed earlier, and it is now convenient to do so, it may be placed at this time, or else, a veil is placed over the head of the wife and the shoulders of the husband, thus symbolizing the bond that unites them.

The Priest says:

Bless, ✠ O Lord, this *lazo* (or: this veil),
a symbol of the indissoluble union
that N. and N. have established from this day forward
before you and with your help.

The *lazo* (or the veil) is held by two family members or friends and is placed over the shoulders of the newly married couple.

THE NUPTIAL BLESSING

72. After the Our Father, the prayer Deliver us is omitted. The Priest, standing and facing the bride and bridegroom, invokes upon them God's blessing, which is never omitted.

In the invitation, if one or both of the spouses will not be receiving Communion, the words in parentheses are omitted.

In the last paragraph of the prayer, the words in parentheses may be omitted if it seems that circumstances suggest it, for example, if the bride and bridegroom are advanced in years.

73. The bride and bridegroom approach the altar or, if appropriate, they remain at their place and kneel.

The Priest, with hands joined, calls upon those present to pray:

Dear brothers and sisters,
let us humbly pray to the Lord
that on these his servants, now married in Christ,
he may mercifully pour out
the blessing of his grace
and make of one heart in love
(by the Sacrament of Christ's Body and Blood)
those he has joined by a holy covenant.

Text with music no. 205A.

Other formulas, nos. 104, 206, 208.

And all pray in silence for a while.

74. Then the Priest, with hands extended over the bride and bridegroom, continues:

O God, who by your mighty power
created all things out of nothing,
and, when you had set in place
the beginnings of the universe,
formed man and woman in your own image,
making the woman an inseparable helpmate to the man,
that they might no longer be two, but one flesh,
and taught that what you were pleased to make one
must never be divided;

O God, who consecrated the bond of Marriage
by so great a mystery
that in the wedding covenant you foreshadowed
the Sacrament of Christ and his Church;

O God, by whom woman is joined to man
and the companionship they had in the beginning
is endowed with the one blessing
not forfeited by original sin
nor washed away by the flood.

Look now with favor on these your servants,
joined together in Marriage,
who ask to be strengthened by your blessing.
Send down on them the grace of the Holy Spirit
and pour your love into their hearts,
that they may remain faithful in the Marriage covenant.

May the grace of love and peace
abide in your daughter N.,
and let her always follow the example of those holy women
whose praises are sung in the Scriptures.

May her husband entrust his heart to her,
so that, acknowledging her as his equal
and his joint heir to the life of grace,
he may show her due honor
and cherish her always
with the love that Christ has for his Church.

And now, Lord, we implore you:
may these your servants
hold fast to the faith and keep your commandments;
made one in the flesh,
may they be blameless in all they do;
and with the strength that comes from the Gospel,
may they bear true witness to Christ before all;
(may they be blessed with children,
and prove themselves virtuous parents,
who live to see their children's children).

And grant that,
reaching at last together the fullness of years
for which they hope,
they may come to the life of the blessed
in the Kingdom of Heaven.
Through Christ our Lord.

℟. Amen.

Text with music no. 205B.

Other formulas for the Nuptial Blessing, nos. 207, 209.

75. The prayer Lord Jesus Christ is omitted, and The peace of the Lord is said immediately. Then the bride and bridegroom and all present offer one another a sign that expresses peace and charity.

76. The bride and bridegroom, their parents, witnesses, and relatives may receive Communion under both kinds.

THE CONCLUSION OF THE CELEBRATION

77. At the end of Mass, the Priest, with hands extended over the bride and bridegroom, says:

May God the eternal Father
keep you of one heart in love for one another,
that the peace of Christ may dwell in you
and abide always in your home.
℟. Amen.

May you be blessed in your children,
have solace in your friends
and enjoy true peace with everyone.
℟. Amen.

May you be witnesses in the world to God's charity,
so that the afflicted and needy
who have known your kindness
may one day receive you thankfully
into the eternal dwelling of God.
℟. Amen.

And he blesses all present, adding:

And may almighty God bless all of you,
who are gathered here,
the Father, and the Son, ✠ and the Holy Spirit.

℟. Amen.

Other formulas, nos. 214-215.

78. When the Mass is concluded, the witnesses and the Priest sign the Marriage record. The signing may take place either in the vesting room or in the presence of the people; however, it is not to be done on the altar.

CHAPTER II

THE ORDER OF CELEBRATING MATRIMONY WITHOUT MASS

79. When Mass is not celebrated, either by necessity or because of circumstances, the order described here is used, even by a Deacon.*

THE INTRODUCTORY RITES

The First Form

80. At the appointed time, the Priest, wearing an alb or surplice, and a white or festive stole, and even a cope (or a dalmatic for a Deacon) of the same color, goes with the servers to the door of the church, receives the bridal party, and warmly greets them, showing that the Church shares in their joy.

81. The procession to the altar then takes place in the customary manner. Meanwhile, the Entrance Chant takes place.

82. The minister approaches the altar, reverences it with a profound bow, and venerates it with a kiss. After this, he goes to the chair.

The Second Form

83. At the appointed time, the Priest, wearing an alb or surplice, a white or festive stole, and even a cope (or a dalmatic for a Deacon) of the same color, goes with the servers to the place prepared for the couple.

84. When the couple have arrived at their place, the minister receives them and warmly greets them, showing that the Church shares in their joy.

85. Then the minister reverences the altar with a profound bow, venerates it with a kiss, and goes to the chair.

---

* Introduction, no. 24.

86. Then, after the Sign of the Cross has been made, he greets those present, saying:

Grace to you and peace from God our Father
and the Lord Jesus Christ.

Or some other suitable greeting, taken from *The Roman Missal.*

All reply:

And with your spirit.

87. Then, in these or similar words, the minister addresses the couple and those present to dispose them inwardly for the celebration of Marriage:

We have come rejoicing into the house of the Lord
for this celebration, dear brothers and sisters,
and now we stand with N. and N.
on the day they intend to form a home of their own.
For them this is a moment of unique importance.
So let us support them
with our affection,
with our friendship,
and with our prayer as their brothers and sisters.
Let us listen attentively with them
to the word that God speaks to us today.
Then, with holy Church,
let us humbly pray to God the Father,
through Christ our Lord,
for this couple, his servants,
that he lovingly accept them,
bless them,
and make them always one.

88. Or:

N. and N., the Church shares your joy
and warmly welcomes you,
together with your families and friends,
as today,
in the presence of God our Father,
you establish between yourselves
a lifelong partnership.
May the Lord hear you on this your joyful day.
May he send you help from heaven and protect you.
May he grant you your hearts' desire
and fulfill every one of your prayers.

89. Then, with hands extended, he says this prayer:

Be attentive to our prayers, O Lord,
and in your kindness
pour out your grace on these your servants (N. and N.),
that, coming together before your altar,
they may be confirmed in love for one another.
Through Christ our Lord.

℟. Amen.

Other prayers, nos. 188, 189, 191, 192, 193.

THE LITURGY OF THE WORD

90. The Liturgy of the Word follows in the usual manner with texts taken from those provided above in no. 56 or with others from the readings indicated below (nos. 144-187).

At least one reading that explicitly speaks of Marriage must always be chosen.

91. Then the minister in the Homily uses the sacred text to expound the mystery of Christian Marriage, the dignity of conjugal love, the grace of the Sacrament, and the responsibilities of married people, keeping in mind, however, the various circumstances of individuals.

THE CELEBRATION OF MATRIMONY

92. If two or more Marriages happen to be celebrated at the same time, the Questions before the Consent, the Consent itself, and also the Reception of the Consent must always take place individually for each Marriage; the remaining parts, however, including the Nuptial Blessing, should be spoken once for all in the plural.

93. With all standing, including the couple and the witnesses, who are positioned near them, the minister addresses the couple in these or similar words:

Dearly beloved,
you have come together into the house of the Church,
so that in the presence of the Church's minister
and the community
your intention to enter into Marriage
may be strengthened by the Lord with a sacred seal.
Christ abundantly blesses the love that binds you.
Through a special Sacrament,
he enriches and strengthens
those he has already consecrated by Holy Baptism,
that they may be faithful to each other for ever
and assume all the responsibilities of married life.
And so, in the presence of the Church,
I ask you to state your intentions.

The Questions before the Consent

94. The minister then questions them about their freedom of choice, fidelity to each other, and the acceptance and upbringing of children, and each responds separately.

N. and N., have you come here to enter into Marriage
without coercion,
freely and wholeheartedly?

The bridegroom and bride each say:

I have.

The minister continues:

Are you prepared, as you follow the path of Marriage,
to love and honor each other
for as long as you both shall live?

The bridegroom and bride each say:

I am.

The following question may be omitted, if circumstances suggest this, for example, if the couple are advanced in years.

Are you prepared to accept children lovingly from God
and to bring them up
according to the law of Christ and his Church?

The bridegroom and bride each say:

I am.

The Consent

95. The minister invites them to declare their consent:

Since it is your intention to enter the covenant
of Holy Matrimony,
join your right hands and declare your consent
before God and his Church.

They join their right hands.

96. The bridegroom says:

I, N., take you, N., to be my wife.
I promise to be faithful to you,
in good times and in bad,
in sickness and in health,
to love you and to honor you
all the days of my life.

The bride says:

I, N., take you, N., to be my husband.
I promise to be faithful to you,
in good times and in bad,
in sickness and in health,
to love you and to honor you
all the days of my life.

The following alternative form may be used:

The bridegroom says:

I, N., take you, N., for my lawful wife,
to have and to hold, from this day forward,
for better, for worse,
for richer, for poorer,
in sickness and in health,
to love and to cherish
until death do us part.

The bride says:

I, N., take you, N., for my lawful husband,
to have and to hold, from this day forward,
for better, for worse,
for richer, for poorer,
in sickness and in health,
to love and to cherish
until death do us part.

---

97. If, however, it seems preferable for pastoral reasons, the minister may obtain the consent of the contracting parties through questioning.

First, he asks the bridegroom:

N., do you take N., to be your wife?
Do you promise to be faithful to her
in good times and in bad,
in sickness and in health,
to love her and to honor her
all the days of your life?

The bridegroom replies:

I do.

Next, the minister asks the bride:

**N., do you take N., to be your husband?
Do you promise to be faithful to him
in good times and in bad,
in sickness and in health,
to love him and to honor him
all the days of your life?**

The bride replies:

I do.

The following alternative form may be used:

First, he asks the bridegroom:

**N., do you take N., for your lawful wife,
to have and to hold, from this day forward,
for better, for worse,
for richer, for poorer,
in sickness and in health,
to love and to cherish
until death do you part?**

The bridegroom replies:

I do.

Next, the minister asks the bride:

**N., do you take N., to be your lawful husband,
to have and to hold, from this day forward,
for better, for worse,
for richer, for poorer,
in sickness and in health,
to love and to cherish
until death do you part?**

The bride replies:

I do.

The Reception of the Consent

98. Then, receiving their consent, the minister says to the bride and bridegroom:

May the Lord in his kindness strengthen the consent
you have declared before the Church,
and graciously bring to fulfillment
his blessing within you.
What God joins together, let no one put asunder.

Or:

May the God of Abraham, the God of Isaac,
the God of Jacob,
the God who joined together our first parents in paradise,
strengthen and bless in Christ
the consent you have declared before the Church,
so that what God joins together, no one may put asunder.

99. The minister invites those present to praise God:

Let us bless the Lord.

All reply:

Thanks be to God.

Another acclamation may be sung or said.

The Blessing and Giving of Rings

100. The minister says:

May the Lord bless ✠ these rings,
which you will give to each other
as a sign of love and fidelity.
℟. Amen.

Other formulas for blessing the rings, nos. 194-195.

He sprinkles the rings, as the circumstances so suggest, and gives them to the bride and bridegroom.

101A. The husband places his wife's ring on her ring finger, saying, as the circumstances so suggest:

N., receive this ring
as a sign of my love and fidelity.
In the name of the Father, and of the Son,
and of the Holy Spirit.

Likewise, the wife places her husband's ring on his ring finger, saying, as the circumstances so suggest:

N., receive this ring
as a sign of my love and fidelity.
In the name of the Father, and of the Son,
and of the Holy Spirit.

THE BLESSING AND GIVING OF THE *ARRAS*

101B. If the occasion so suggests, the rite of blessing and giving of the *arras* (coins) may take place following the blessing and giving of rings.

The minister says:

Bless, ✠ O Lord, these *arras*
that N. and N. will give to each other
and pour over them the abundance of
your good gifts.

The husband takes the *arras* and hands them over to his wife, saying:

N., receive these *arras* as a pledge of God's blessing
and a sign of the good gifts we will share.

The wife takes the *arras* and hands them over to the husband, saying:

N., receive these *arras* as a pledge of God's blessing
and a sign of the good gifts we will share.

---

102. Then a hymn or canticle of praise may be sung by the whole community.

The Universal Prayer

103A. The Universal Prayer then takes place (examples are provided in nos. 216-217):

a) first, the minister says the invitation to prayer;

b) the invocations of the Universal Prayer with the response of the faithful follow, but in such a way that the individual invocations should be consistent with the Nuptial Blessing, yet should not duplicate it;

c) if Holy Communion is not to be distributed, the Lord's Prayer follows;

d) then the concluding prayer is omitted and the minister invokes upon the bride and bridegroom God's blessing, which is never omitted.

The Blessing and Placing of the *Lazo* or the Veil

103B. According to local customs, the rite of blessing and imposition of the *lazo* (wedding garland) or of the veil may take place before the Nuptial Blessing. The spouses remain at their place and kneel. Then, if it is convenient to do so, the *lazo* may be placed at this time, or else, a veil is placed over the head of the wife and the shoulders of the husband, thus symbolizing the bond that unites them.

The minister says:

Bless, ✠ O Lord, this *lazo* (or: this veil),
a symbol of the indissoluble union
that N. and N. have established from this day forward
before you and with your help.

The *lazo* (or the veil) is held by two family members or friends and is placed over the shoulders of the newly married couple.

The Nuptial Blessing

104. The bride and bridegroom remain at their place and kneel.

Then, the minister, with hands joined, continues:

Now let us humbly invoke God's blessing
upon this bride and groom,
that in his kindness he may favor with his help
those on whom he has bestowed
the Sacrament of Matrimony.

Text with music, no. 205A.

Other formulas, nos. 73, 206.

And all pray in silence for a while.

105. Then the minister, standing and turned toward the bride and bridegroom with hands extended over them, says the following prayer.

In the last paragraph of the prayer, the words in parentheses may be omitted if it seems that circumstances suggest it, for example, if the bride and bridegroom are advanced in years.

O God, who by your mighty power
created all things out of nothing,
and, when you had set in place
the beginnings of the universe,
formed man and woman in your own image,
making the woman an inseparable helpmate to the man,
that they might no longer be two, but one flesh,
and taught that what you were pleased to make one
must never be divided;

O God, who consecrated the bond of Marriage
by so great a mystery
that in the wedding covenant you foreshadowed
the Sacrament of Christ and his Church;

O God, by whom woman is joined to man
and the companionship they had in the beginning
is endowed with the one blessing
not forfeited by original sin
nor washed away by the flood.

Look now with favor on these your servants,
joined together in Marriage,
who ask to be strengthened by your blessing.
Send down on them the grace of the Holy Spirit
and pour your love into their hearts,
that they may remain faithful in the Marriage covenant.

**May the grace of love and peace
abide in your daughter N.,
and let her always follow the example
of those holy women
whose praises are sung in the Scriptures.**

**May her husband entrust his heart to her,
so that, acknowledging her as his equal
and his joint heir to the life of grace,
he may show her due honor
and cherish her always
with the love that Christ has for his Church.**

**And now, Lord, we implore you:
may these your servants
hold fast to the faith and keep your commandments;
made one in the flesh,
may they be blameless in all they do;
and with the strength that comes from the Gospel,
may they bear true witness to Christ before all;
(may they be blessed with children,
and prove themselves virtuous parents,
who live to see their children's children).**

**And grant that,
reaching at last together the fullness of years
for which they hope,
they may come to the life of the blessed
in the Kingdom of Heaven.
Through Christ our Lord.**

℟. Amen.

Text with music, no. 205B.

Other formulas for the Nuptial Blessing, nos. 207, 209.

106. Then, if Holy Communion is not to be distributed, the minister immediately blesses the people, saying:

May almighty God bless all of you,
who are gathered here,
the Father, and the Son, ✠ and the Holy Spirit.

℟. Amen.

107. It is a praiseworthy practice to end the celebration with a suitable chant.

Holy Communion

108. If Holy Communion is to be distributed, after the Nuptial Blessing, the minister approaches the place where the Eucharist is reserved, takes the vessel or ciborium with the Body of the Lord, places it on the altar, and genuflects.

109. Then, he introduces the Lord's Prayer:

At the Savior's command
and formed by divine teaching,
we dare to say:

And all continue together:

Our Father, who art in heaven,
hallowed be thy name;
thy kingdom come,
thy will be done
on earth as it is in heaven.
Give us this day our daily bread,
and forgive us our trespasses,
as we forgive those who trespass against us;
and lead us not into temptation,
but deliver us from evil.

110. After this, if appropriate, the minister invites the faithful:

Let us offer each other the sign of peace.

Then the bride and bridegroom and all present offer one another a sign that expresses peace and charity.

111. When this has been completed, the minister genuflects, takes a host and, holding it slightly raised above the vessel or ciborium, while facing the communicants, says:

Behold the Lamb of God,
behold him who takes away the sins of the world.
Blessed are those called to the supper of the Lamb.

The communicants say together:

Lord, I am not worthy
that you should enter under my roof,
but only say the word
and my soul shall be healed.

112. After this, the minister approaches the communicants, raises a host slightly and shows it to each of them, saying:

The Body of Christ.

The communicant replies:

Amen.

And receives Holy Communion.

113. During the distribution of Communion, a suitable chant, if appropriate, may be sung.

114. When the distribution of Communion is over, if appropriate, sacred silence may be observed for a while, or a psalm or canticle of praise may be sung.

115. Then the minister says this prayer:

Let us pray.

Having been made partakers at your table,
we pray, O Lord,
that those who are united by the Sacrament of Marriage
may always hold fast to you
and proclaim your name to the world.
Through Christ our Lord.

℟. Amen.

THE CONCLUSION OF THE CELEBRATION

116. The rite concludes with the blessing of the bride and bridegroom and the people, either with the simple form May almighty God bless you, or with one of the formulas provided below, nos. 213-215.

117. When the celebration is concluded, the witnesses and the minister sign the Marriage record. The signing may take place either in the vesting room or in the presence of the people; however, it is not to be done on the altar.

DOMINVS
ET BENEDICTVS

CHAPTER III

THE ORDER OF CELEBRATING MATRIMONY BETWEEN A CATHOLIC AND A CATECHUMEN OR A NON-CHRISTIAN

118. When Marriage is contracted by a Catholic and a catechumen or a non-Christian, the celebration takes place in a church or in another suitable place, according to the following rite.

The order provided here is to be observed by a Priest or by a Deacon who has received delegation from the local Ordinary or the pastor to assist at the celebration of Marriages and to bless them in the name of the Church.

THE RITE OF RECEPTION

119. At the appointed time, the Priest or Deacon, wearing an alb and stole, and even a cope (or a dalmatic, for a Deacon) of the color white or a festive color, goes with the servers to the door of the church or to the place that has been chosen, where he receives the bridal party and warmly greets them.

After this, the one who presides, the servers, the couple, the witnesses, and all present go to the seats prepared for each one.

120. Then, in these or similar words, the one who presides addresses them to dispose them inwardly for the celebration of Marriage:

N. and N., the Church shares your joy
and warmly welcomes you,
together with your families and friends,
as today you establish between yourselves
a lifelong partnership.
For believers God is the source of love and fidelity,
because God is love.
So let us listen attentively to his word,
and let us humbly pray to him,
that he may grant you your hearts' desire
and fulfill every one of your prayers.

121. If, however, circumstances so suggest, the Rite of Reception is omitted and the celebration of Marriage begins with the Liturgy of the Word.

THE LITURGY OF THE WORD

122. The Liturgy of the Word follows in the usual manner with texts taken from those provided above in no. 56 or with others from the readings indicated below (nos. 144-187). There may be one or two readings. If, however, circumstances make this more desirable, there may be only one reading. At least one reading that explicitly speaks of Marriage must always be chosen.

123. After this, there should be a homily on the sacred text, which should be adapted to the responsibilities and situation of the couple and other circumstances.

THE CELEBRATION OF MATRIMONY

124. Then, with all standing, including the couple and the witnesses, who are positioned near them, the one who presides addresses the couple in these or similar words:

Dearly beloved,
you have come together here
before a minister of the Church
and in the presence of the community
so that your intention to enter into Marriage
may be strengthened by the Lord with a sacred seal,
and your love be enriched with his blessing,
so that you may have strength
to be faithful to each other for ever
and to assume all the responsibilities of married life.
And so, in the presence of the Church,
I ask you to state your intentions.

The Questions before the Consent

125. The one who presides then questions them about their freedom of choice, fidelity to each other, and the acceptance and upbringing of children, and each responds separately.

N. and N., have you come here to enter into Marriage without coercion, freely and wholeheartedly?

The bridegroom and bride each say:

I have.

The one who presides continues:

Are you prepared, as you follow the path of Marriage,
to love and honor each other
for as long as you both shall live?

The bridegroom and bride each say:

I am.

The following question may be omitted, if circumstances suggest this, for example, if the couple are advanced in years.

Are you prepared to accept children lovingly from God
and to bring them up
according to the law of Christ and his Church?

The bridegroom and bride each say:

I am.

The Consent

126. The one who presides invites them to declare their consent:

Since it is your intention to enter the covenant
of Holy Matrimony,
join your right hands and declare your consent
before God and his Church.

They join their right hands.

127. The bridegroom says:

I, N., take you, N., to be my wife.
I promise to be faithful to you,
in good times and in bad,
in sickness and in health,
to love you and to honor you
all the days of my life.

The bride says:

I, N., take you, N., to be my husband.
I promise to be faithful to you,
in good times and in bad,
in sickness and in health,
to love you and to honor you
all the days of my life.

The following alternative form may be used:

The bridegroom says:

I, N., take you, N., for my lawful wife,
to have and to hold, from this day forward,
for better, for worse,
for richer, for poorer,
in sickness and in health,
to love and to cherish
until death do us part.

The bride says:

I, N., take you, N., for my lawful husband,
to have and to hold, from this day forward,
for better, for worse,
for richer, for poorer,
in sickness and in health,
to love and to cherish
until death do us part.

---

128. If, however, it seems preferable for pastoral reasons, the one who presides may obtain the consent of the contracting parties through questioning.

First, the one who presides asks the bridegroom:

**N., do you take N., to be your wife?
Do you promise to be faithful to her
in good times and in bad,
in sickness and in health,
to love her and to honor her
all the days of your life?**

The bridegroom replies:

I do.

Next, the one who presides asks the bride:

**N., do you take N., to be your husband?
Do you promise to be faithful to him
in good times and in bad,
in sickness and in health,
to love him and to honor him
all the days of your life?**

The bride replies:

I do.

The following alternative form may be used:

First, the one who presides asks the bridegroom:

**N., do you take N. for your lawful wife,
to have and to hold, from this day forward,
for better, for worse,
for richer, for poorer,
in sickness and in health,
to love and to cherish
until death do you part?**

The bridegroom replies:

I do.

Next, the one who presides asks the bride:

N., do you take N. for your lawful husband,
to have and to hold, from this day forward,
for better, for worse,
for richer, for poorer,
in sickness and in health,
to love and to cherish
until death do you part?

The bride replies:

I do.

The Reception of the Consent

129. Then, receiving their consent, the one who presides says to the bride and bridegroom:

May the Lord in his kindness strengthen the consent
you have declared before the Church,
and graciously bring to fulfillment
his blessing within you.
What God joins together, let no one put asunder.

Or:

May the God of Abraham, the God of Isaac,
the God of Jacob,
the God who joined together our first parents in paradise,
strengthen and bless in Christ
the consent you have declared before the Church,
so that what God joins together, no one may put asunder.

130. The one who presides invites all present to praise God:

Let us bless the Lord.

All reply:

Thanks be to God.

Another acclamation may be sung or said.

The Blessing and Giving of Rings

131. If circumstances so suggest, the blessing and giving of rings may be omitted. If they are included, however, the Priest (or Deacon), says:

May the Lord bless ✠ these rings,
which you will give to each other
as a sign of love and fidelity.

℟. Amen.

Other formulas for blessing the rings, nos. 194-195.

The one who presides sprinkles the rings, if appropriate, and gives them to the bride and bridegroom.

132. The husband places his wife's ring on her ring finger, saying, if appropriate:

N., receive this ring
as a sign of my love and fidelity.

If he is a Christian, he may add:

In the name of the Father, and of the Son,
and of the Holy Spirit.

Likewise, the wife places her husband's ring on his ring finger, saying, if appropriate:

N., receive this ring
as a sign of my love and fidelity.

If she is a Christian, she may add:

In the name of the Father, and of the Son,
and of the Holy Spirit.

THE BLESSING AND GIVING OF THE *ARRAS*

133. If the occasion so suggests, the rite of blessing and giving of the *arras* (coins) may take place following the blessing and giving of rings.

The one who presides says:

Bless, ✠ O Lord, these *arras*
that N. and N. will give to each other
and pour over them the abundance of
your good gifts.

The husband takes the *arras* and hands them over to his wife, saying:

N., receive these *arras* as a pledge of God's blessing
and a sign of the good gifts we will share.

The wife takes the *arras* and hands them over to the husband, saying:

N., receive these *arras* as a pledge of God's blessing
and a sign of the good gifts we will share.

---

134. Then a hymn or canticle of praise may be sung by the whole community.

THE UNIVERSAL PRAYER

135. After this, the Universal Prayer takes place (examples are provided in nos. 216-217).

136. After the invocations, the one who presides continues:

God the Father wills that his children be
of one heart in charity;
let those who are Christian call upon him
in the prayer of God's family,
which our Lord Jesus Christ has taught us:

And all the Christians continue:

Our Father, who art in heaven,
hallowed be thy name;
thy kingdom come,
thy will be done
on earth as it is in heaven.
Give us this day our daily bread,
and forgive us our trespasses,
as we forgive those who trespass against us;
and lead us not into temptation,
but deliver us from evil.

The Blessing and Placing of the *Lazo* or the Veil

137. According to local customs, the rite of blessing and imposition of the *lazo* (wedding garland) or of the veil may take place before the Nuptial Blessing. The spouses remain at their place and kneel. Then, if it is convenient to do so, the *lazo* may be placed at this time, or else, a veil is placed over the head of the wife and the shoulders of the husband, thus symbolizing the bond that unites them.

The one who presides says:

Bless, ✠ O Lord, this *lazo* (or: this veil),
a symbol of the indissoluble union
that N. and N. have established from this day forward
before you and with your help.

The *lazo* (or the veil) is held by two family members or friends and is placed over the shoulders of the newly married couple.

The Nuptial Blessing

138. As a rule, the Nuptial Blessing is said over the bride and bridegroom. Nevertheless, if circumstances suggest this, it may be omitted and, in this case, the prayer provided in no. 140 is said in place of the Nuptial Blessing.

The bride and bridegroom kneel at their place, if circumstances suggest this.

Then, the one who presides continues, with hands joined:

Now let us humbly invoke God's blessing
upon this bride and groom,
that in his kindness he may favor with his help
those on whom he has bestowed the bond of Marriage.

And all pray in silence for a while.

139. Then the one who presides, standing and turned toward the bride and bridegroom with hands extended over them, continues:

Holy Father, maker of the whole world,
who created man and woman in your own image
and willed that their union be crowned
with your blessing,
we humbly beseech you for these your servants,
who are joined today in the Marriage covenant.

May your abundant blessing, Lord,
come down upon this bride, N.,
and upon N., her companion for life,
and may the power of your Holy Spirit
set their hearts aflame from on high,
so that, living out together the gift of Matrimony,
they may be known for the integrity of their conduct
(and be recognized as virtuous parents).

In happiness may they praise you, O Lord,
in sorrow may they seek you out;
may they have the joy of your presence
to assist them in their toil,
and know that you are near
to comfort them in their need;
and after a happy old age,
together with the circle of friends that surrounds them,
may they come to the Kingdom of Heaven.
Through Christ our Lord.

℟. Amen.

140. If, because of circumstances, the Nuptial Blessing is omitted, this prayer is spoken over the bride and bridegroom:

Be attentive to our prayers, O Lord,
and in your kindness uphold
what you have established for the increase
of the human race,
so that the union you have created
may be kept safe by your assistance.
Through Christ our Lord.

℟. Amen.

THE CONCLUSION OF THE CELEBRATION

141. Then, the one who presides blesses the people, saying:

May almighty God bless all of you,
who are gathered here,
the Father, and the Son, ✠ and the Holy Spirit.

℟. Amen.

142. It is a praiseworthy practice to end the celebration with a suitable chant.

143. When the celebration is concluded, the witnesses and the one who presides sign the Marriage record. The signing may take place either in the vesting room or in the presence of the people; however, it is not to be done on the altar.

CHAPTER IV

VARIOUS TEXTS TO BE USED IN THE RITE OF MARRIAGE AND IN THE MASS FOR THE CELEBRATION OF MARRIAGE

I. BIBLICAL READINGS

The passages that follow may be used in the Mass "For the Celebration of Marriage" and in the celebration of Marriages without Mass. At least one reading that explicitly speaks of Marriage must always be chosen. These readings are designated by an asterisk.

Readings from the Old Testament

Readings from the New Testament

Responsorial Psalms

Alleluia Verses and Verses before the Gospel

Gospel Readings

Readings from the Old Testament

(*Lectionary for Mass*, no. 801)

*144.

1

Genesis 1:26-28, 31a

A reading from the Book of Genesis

Male and female he created them.

Then God said:
"Let us make man in our image, after our likeness.
Let them have dominion over the fish of the sea,
the birds of the air, and the cattle,
and over all the wild animals
and all the creatures that crawl on the ground."

God created man in his image;
in the image of God he created him;
male and female he created them.

God blessed them, saying:
"Be fertile and multiply;
fill the earth and subdue it.
Have dominion over the fish of the sea, the birds of the air,
and all the living things that move on the earth."
God looked at everything he had made, and he found it very good.

The word of the Lord.

*145.

2

Genesis 2:18-24

A reading from the Book of Genesis

The two of them become one body.

The LORD God said: "It is not good for the man to be alone.
I will make a suitable partner for him."
So the LORD God formed out of the ground
various wild animals and various birds of the air,
and he brought them to the man to see what he would call them;
whatever the man called each of them would be its name.
The man gave names to all the cattle,
all the birds of the air, and all wild animals;
but none proved to be the suitable partner for the man.

So the LORD God cast a deep sleep on the man,
and while he was asleep,
he took out one of his ribs and closed up its place with flesh.
The LORD God then built up into a woman the rib
that he had taken from the man.
When he brought her to the man, the man said:

"This one, at last, is bone of my bones
and flesh of my flesh;
This one shall be called 'woman,'
for out of 'her man' this one has been taken."

That is why a man leaves his father and mother
and clings to his wife,
and the two of them become one body.

The word of the Lord.

*146.

3

Genesis 24:48-51, 58-67

A reading from the Book of Genesis

In his love for Rebekah, Isaac found solace after the death of his mother.

The servant of Abraham said to Laban:
"I bowed down in worship to the LORD,
blessing the LORD, the God of my master Abraham,
who had led me on the right road
to obtain the daughter of my master's kinsman for his son.
If, therefore, you have in mind to show true loyalty to my master,
let me know;
but if not, let me know that, too.
I can then proceed accordingly."

Laban and his household said in reply:
"This thing comes from the LORD;
we can say nothing to you either for or against it.
Here is Rebekah, ready for you;
take her with you,
that she may become the wife of your master's son,
as the LORD has said."

So they called Rebekah and asked her,
"Do you wish to go with this man?"
She answered, "I do."
At this they allowed their sister Rebekah and her nurse to take leave,
along with Abraham's servant and his men.
Invoking a blessing on Rebekah, they said:

"Sister, may you grow
into thousands of myriads;
And may your descendants gain possession
of the gates of their enemies!"

Then Rebekah and her maids started out;
they mounted their camels and followed the man.
So the servant took Rebekah and went on his way.

Meanwhile Isaac had gone from Beer-lahai-roi
and was living in the region of the Negeb.
One day toward evening he went out . . . in the field,
and as he looked around, he noticed that camels were approaching.
Rebekah, too, was looking about, and when she saw him,
she alighted from her camel and asked the servant,
"Who is the man out there, walking through the fields toward us?"
"That is my master," replied the servant.
Then she covered herself with her veil.

The servant recounted to Isaac all the things he had done.
Then Isaac took Rebekah into his tent;
he married her, and thus she became his wife.
In his love for her Isaac found solace
after the death of his mother Sarah.

The word of the Lord.

*147.

4

Tobit 7:6-14

A reading from the Book of Tobit

May the Lord of heaven prosper you both.
May he grant you mercy and peace.

Raphael and Tobiah entered the house of Raguel and greeted him.
Raguel sprang up and kissed Tobiah, shedding tears of joy.
But when he heard that Tobit had lost his eyesight,
he was grieved and wept aloud.
He said to Tobiah:
"My child, God bless you!
You are the son of a noble and good father.
But what a terrible misfortune
that such a righteous and charitable man
should be afflicted with blindness!"
He continued to weep in the arms of his kinsman Tobiah.
His wife Edna also wept for Tobit;
and even their daughter Sarah began to weep.

Afterward, Raguel slaughtered a ram from the flock
and gave them a cordial reception.
When they had bathed and reclined to eat,
Tobiah said to Raphael, "Brother Azariah,
ask Raguel to let me marry my kinswoman Sarah."
Raguel overheard the words;
so he said to the boy:
"Eat and drink and be merry tonight,
for no man is more entitled to marry my daughter Sarah
than you, brother.

Besides, not even I have the right to give her to anyone but you,
because you are my closest relative.
But I will explain the situation to you very frankly.
I have given her in marriage to seven men,
all of whom were kinsmen of ours,
and all died on the very night they approached her.
But now, son, eat and drink.
I am sure the Lord will look after you both."
Tobiah answered, "I will eat or drink nothing
until you set aside what belongs to me."

Raguel said to him: "I will do it.
She is yours according to the decree of the Book of Moses.
Your marriage to her has been decided in heaven!
Take your kinswoman
from now on you are her love,
and she is your beloved.
She is yours today and ever after.
And tonight, son, may the Lord of heaven prosper you both.
May he grant you mercy and peace."
Then Raguel called his daughter Sarah, and she came to him.
He took her by the hand and gave her to Tobiah with the words:
"Take her according to the law.
According to the decree written in the Book of Moses she is your wife.
Take her and bring her back safely to your father.
And may the God of heaven grant both of you peace and prosperity."

**He then called her mother and told her to bring a scroll,
so that he might draw up a marriage contract
stating that he gave Sarah to Tobiah as his wife
according to the decree of the Mosaic law.
Her mother brought the scroll,
and he drew up the contract,
to which they affixed their seal.**

Afterward they began to eat and drink.

The word of the Lord.

*148.

5

Tobit 8:4b-8

A reading from the Book of Tobit

Allow us to live together to a happy old age.

**On their wedding night Tobiah arose from bed and said to his wife,
"Sister, get up. Let us pray and beg our Lord
to have mercy on us and to grant us deliverance."
Sarah got up, and they started to pray
and beg that deliverance might be theirs.
They began with these words:**

**"Blessed are you, O God of our fathers;
praised be your name forever and ever.
Let the heavens and all your creation
praise you forever.
You made Adam and you gave him his wife Eve
to be his help and support;
and from these two the human race descended.
You said, 'It is not good for the man to be alone;
let us make him a partner like himself.'**

Now, Lord, you know that I take this wife of mine
not because of lust,
but for a noble purpose.
Call down your mercy on me and on her,
and allow us to live together to a happy old age."

They said together, "Amen, Amen."

The word of the Lord.

*149.

6

Proverbs 31:10-13, 19-20, 30-31

A reading from the Book of Proverbs

The woman who fears the LORD is to be praised.

When one finds a worthy wife,
her value is far beyond pearls.
Her husband, entrusting his heart to her,
has an unfailing prize.
She brings him good, and not evil,
all the days of her life.
She obtains wool and flax
and makes cloth with skillful hands.
She puts her hands to the distaff,
and her fingers ply the spindle.
She reaches out her hands to the poor,
and extends her arms to the needy.
Charm is deceptive and beauty fleeting;
the woman who fears the LORD is to be praised.
Give her a reward of her labors,
and let her works praise her at the city gates.

The word of the Lord.

150.

7

Song of Songs 2:8-10, 14, 16a; 8:6-7a

A reading from the Song of Songs

Stern as death is love.

Hark! my lover—here he comes
springing across the mountains,
leaping across the hills.
My lover is like a gazelle
or a young stag.
Here he stands behind our wall,
gazing through the windows,
peering through the lattices.
My lover speaks; he says to me,
"Arise, my beloved, my dove, my beautiful one, and come!

"O my dove in the clefts of the rock,
in the secret recesses of the cliff,
Let me see you,
let me hear your voice,
For your voice is sweet,
and you are lovely."

My lover belongs to me and I to him.
He says to me:

"Set me as a seal on your heart,
as a seal on your arm;
For stern as death is love,
relentless as the nether world is devotion;
its flames are a blazing fire.
Deep waters cannot quench love,
nor floods sweep it away."

The word of the Lord.

*151.

8

Sirach 26:1-4, 13-16 (Vg. 26:1-4, 16-21)

A reading from the Book of Sirach

Like the sun rising in the LORD's heavens,
the beauty of a virtuous wife is the radiance of her home.

Blessed the husband of a good wife,
twice-lengthened are his days;
A worthy wife brings joy to her husband,
peaceful and full is his life.
A good wife is a generous gift
bestowed upon him who fears the LORD;
Be he rich or poor, his heart is content,
and a smile is ever on his face.

A gracious wife delights her husband,
her thoughtfulness puts flesh on his bones;
A gift from the LORD is her governed speech,
and her firm virtue is of surpassing worth.
Choicest of blessings is a modest wife,
priceless her chaste soul.
A holy and decent woman adds grace upon grace;
indeed, no price is worthy of her temperate soul.
Like the sun rising in the LORD's heavens,
the beauty of a virtuous wife is the radiance of her home.

The word of the Lord.

152.

9 Jeremiah 31:31-32a, 33-34a

A reading from the Book of the Prophet Jeremiah

I will make a new covenant with the house of Israel and the house of Judah.

The days are coming, says the LORD,
when I will make a new covenant with the house of Israel
and the house of Judah.
It will not be like the covenant I made with their fathers:
the day I took them by the hand
to lead them forth from the land of Egypt.
But this is the covenant which I will make
with the house of Israel after those days, says the LORD.
I will place my law within them, and write it upon their hearts;
I will be their God, and they shall be my people.
No longer will they have need to teach their friends and relatives
how to know the LORD.
All, from least to greatest, shall know me, says the LORD.

The word of the Lord.

Readings from the New Testament

(*Lectionary for Mass*, no. 802)

153.

1 Romans 8:31b-35, 37-39

A reading from the Letter of Saint Paul to the Romans

What will separate us from the love of Christ?

Brothers and sisters:
If God is for us, who can be against us?
He did not spare his own Son
but handed him over for us all,
how will he not also give us everything else along with him?
Who will bring a charge against God's chosen ones?
It is God who acquits us.
Who will condemn?
It is Christ Jesus who died, rather, was raised,
who also is at the right hand of God,
who indeed intercedes for us.
What will separate us from the love of Christ?
Will anguish, or distress, or persecution, or famine,
or nakedness, or peril, or the sword?
No, in all these things, we conquer overwhelmingly
through him who loved us.
For I am convinced that neither death, nor life,
nor angels, nor principalities,
nor present things, nor future things,
nor powers, nor height, nor depth,
nor any other creature will be able to separate us
from the love of God in Christ Jesus our Lord.

The word of the Lord.

154.

2 Romans 12:1-2, 9-18

LONG FORM

A reading from the Letter of Saint Paul to the Romans

Offer your bodies as a living sacrifice, holy and pleasing to God.

I urge you, brothers and sisters, by the mercies of God,
to offer your bodies as a living sacrifice,
holy and pleasing to God, your spiritual worship.
Do not conform yourselves to this age
but be transformed by the renewal of your mind,
that you may discern what is the will of God,
what is good and pleasing and perfect.

Let love be sincere;
hate what is evil,
hold on to what is good;
love one another with mutual affection;
anticipate one another in showing honor.
Do not grow slack in zeal,
be fervent in spirit,
serve the Lord.
Rejoice in hope,
endure in affliction,
persevere in prayer.
Contribute to the needs of the holy ones,
exercise hospitality.
Bless those who persecute you,
bless and do not curse them.
Rejoice with those who rejoice,
weep with those who weep.
Have the same regard for one another;
do not be haughty but associate with the lowly;
do not be wise in your own estimation.

Do not repay anyone evil for evil;
be concerned for what is noble in the sight of all.
If possible, on your part, live at peace with all.

The word of the Lord.

OR

SHORT FORM Romans 12:1-2, 9-13

A reading from the Letter of Saint Paul to the Romans

Offer your bodies as a living sacrifice, holy and pleasing to God.

I urge you, brothers and sisters, by the mercies of God,
to offer your bodies as a living sacrifice,
holy and pleasing to God, your spiritual worship.
Do not conform yourselves to this age
but be transformed by the renewal of your mind,
that you may discern what is the will of God,
what is good and pleasing and perfect.

Let love be sincere;
hate what is evil,
hold on to what is good;
love one another with mutual affection;
anticipate one another in showing honor.
Do not grow slack in zeal,
be fervent in spirit,
serve the Lord.
Rejoice in hope,
endure in affliction,
persevere in prayer.
Contribute to the needs of the holy ones,
exercise hospitality.

The word of the Lord.

155.

3

Romans 15:1b-3a, 5-7, 13

A reading from the Letter of Saint Paul to the Romans

Welcome one another as Christ welcomed you.

Brothers and sisters:
We ought to put up with the failings of the weak and not to please ourselves;
let each of us please our neighbor for the good,
for building up.
For Christ did not please himself.
May the God of endurance and encouragement
grant you to think in harmony with one another,
in keeping with Christ Jesus,
that with one accord you may with one voice
glorify the God and Father of our Lord Jesus Christ.

Welcome one another, then, as Christ welcomed you,
for the glory of God.
May the God of hope fill you with all joy and peace in believing,
so that you may abound in hope by the power of the Holy Spirit.

The word of the Lord.

156.

4

1 Corinthians 6:13c-15a, 17-20

A reading from the first Letter of Saint Paul to the Corinthians

Your body is a temple of the Spirit.

Brothers and sisters:
The body is not for immorality, but for the Lord,
and the Lord is for the body;
God raised the Lord and will also raise us by his power.

Do you not know that your bodies are members of Christ?
Whoever is joined to the Lord becomes one spirit with him.
Avoid immorality.
Every other sin a person commits is outside the body,
but the immoral person sins against his own body.
Do you not know that your body
is a temple of the Holy Spirit within you,
whom you have from God, and that you are not your own?
For you have been purchased at a price.
Therefore glorify God in your body.

The word of the Lord.

157.

5

1 Corinthians 12:31—13:8a

A reading from the first Letter of Saint Paul to the Corinthians

If I do not have love, I gain nothing.

**Brothers and sisters:
Strive eagerly for the greatest spiritual gifts.**

**But I shall show you a still more excellent way.
If I speak in human and angelic tongues
but do not have love,
I am a resounding gong or a clashing cymbal.
And if I have the gift of prophecy
and comprehend all mysteries and all knowledge;
if I have all faith so as to move mountains,
but do not have love, I am nothing.
If I give away everything I own,
and if I hand my body over so that I may boast
but do not have love, I gain nothing.**

**Love is patient, love is kind.
It is not jealous, is not pompous,
it is not inflated, it is not rude,
it does not seek its own interests,
it is not quick-tempered, it does not brood over injury,
it does not rejoice over wrongdoing
but rejoices with the truth.
It bears all things, believes all things,
hopes all things, endures all things.
Love never fails.**

The word of the Lord.

158.

6 Ephesians 4:1-6

A reading from the Letter of Saint Paul to the Ephesians

One Body and one Spirit.†

Brothers and sisters:
I, a prisoner for the Lord,
urge you to live in a manner worthy of the call you have received,
with all humility and gentleness, with patience,
bearing with one another through love,
striving to preserve the unity of the Spirit
through the bond of peace: one Body and one Spirit,
as you were also called to the one hope of your call;
one Lord, one faith, one baptism;
one God and Father of all,
who is over all and through all and in all.

The word of the Lord.

†Cf. *Lectionary for Mass*, no. 807-2.

*159.

Ephesians 5:2a, 21-33

LONG FORM

A reading from the Letter of Saint Paul to the Ephesians

This is a great mystery, but I speak in reference to Christ and the Church.

**Brothers and sisters:
Live in love, as Christ loved us
and handed himself over for us.**

**Be subordinate to one another out of reverence for Christ.
Wives should be subordinate to their husbands as to the Lord.
For the husband is head of his wife
just as Christ is head of the Church,
he himself the savior of the body.
As the Church is subordinate to Christ,
so wives should be subordinate to their husbands in everything.
Husbands, love your wives,
even as Christ loved the Church
and handed himself over for her to sanctify her,
cleansing her by the bath of water with the word,
that he might present to himself the Church in splendor,
without spot or wrinkle or any such thing,
that she might be holy and without blemish.**

So also husbands should love their wives as their own bodies.
He who loves his wife loves himself.
For no one hates his own flesh
but rather nourishes and cherishes it,
even as Christ does the Church,
because we are members of his Body.

For this reason a man shall leave his father and his mother
and be joined to his wife,
and the two shall become one flesh.

This is a great mystery,
but I speak in reference to Christ and the Church.
In any case, each one of you should love his wife as himself,
and the wife should respect her husband.

The word of the Lord.

OR

SHORT FORM Ephesians 5:2a, 25-32

A reading from the Letter of Saint Paul to the Ephesians

This is a great mystery, but I speak in reference to Christ and the Church.

Brothers and sisters:
Live in love, as Christ loved us
and handed himself over for us.

Husbands, love your wives,
even as Christ loved the Church
and handed himself over for her to sanctify her,
cleansing her by the bath of water with the word,
that he might present to himself the Church in splendor,
without spot or wrinkle or any such thing,
that she might be holy and without blemish.
So also husbands should love their wives as their own bodies.
He who loves his wife loves himself.
For no one hates his own flesh
but rather nourishes and cherishes it,
even as Christ does the Church,
because we are members of his Body.

For this reason a man shall leave his father and his mother
and be joined to his wife,
and the two shall become one flesh.

This is a great mystery,
but I speak in reference to Christ and the Church.

The word of the Lord.

160.

8

Philippians 4:4-9

A reading from the Letter of Saint Paul to the Philippians

The God of peace will be with you.

Brothers and sisters:
Rejoice in the Lord always.
I shall say it again: rejoice!
Your kindness should be known to all.
The Lord is near.
Have no anxiety at all, but in everything,
by prayer and petition, with thanksgiving,
make your requests known to God.
Then the peace of God that surpasses all understanding
will guard your hearts and minds in Christ Jesus.

Finally, brothers and sisters,
whatever is true, whatever is honorable,
whatever is just, whatever is pure,
whatever is lovely, whatever is gracious,
if there is any excellence
and if there is anything worthy of praise,
think about these things.
Keep on doing what you have learned and received
and heard and seen in me.
Then the God of peace will be with you.

The word of the Lord.

161.

9 Colossians 3:12-17

A reading from the Letter of Saint Paul to the Colossians

And over all these put on love,
that is, the bond of perfection.

Brothers and sisters:
Put on, as God's chosen ones, holy and beloved,
heartfelt compassion, kindness, humility, gentleness,
and patience,
bearing with one another and forgiving one another,
if one has a grievance against another;
as the Lord has forgiven you, so must you also do.
And over all these put on love,
that is, the bond of perfection.
And let the peace of Christ control your hearts,
the peace into which you were also called in one Body.
And be thankful.
Let the word of Christ dwell in you richly,
as in all wisdom you teach and admonish one another,
singing psalms, hymns, and spiritual songs
with gratitude in your hearts to God.
And whatever you do, in word or in deed,
do everything in the name of the Lord Jesus,
giving thanks to God the Father through him.

The word of the Lord.

162.

10

Hebrews 13:1-4a, 5-6b

A reading from the Letter to the Hebrews

Let marriage be held in honor by all.

Brothers and sisters:
Let mutual love continue.
Do not neglect hospitality,
for through it some have unknowingly entertained angels.
Be mindful of prisoners as if sharing their imprisonment,
and of the ill-treated as of yourselves,
for you also are in the body.
Let marriage be honored among all
and the marriage bed be kept undefiled.
Let your life be free from love of money
but be content with what you have,
for he has said, *I will never forsake you or abandon you.*
Thus we may say with confidence:

The Lord is my helper,
and I will not be afraid.

The word of the Lord.

*163.

11

1 Peter 3:1-9

A reading from the first Letter of Saint Peter

Be of one mind, sympathetic, loving toward one another.

Beloved:
You wives should be subordinate to your husbands so that,
even if some disobey the word,
they may be won over without a word by their wives' conduct
when they observe your reverent and chaste behavior.
Your adornment should not be an external one:
braiding the hair, wearing gold jewelry, or dressing in fine clothes,
but rather the hidden character of the heart,
expressed in the imperishable beauty
of a gentle and calm disposition,
which is precious in the sight of God.
For this is also how the holy women who hoped in God
once used to adorn themselves
and were subordinate to their husbands;
thus Sarah obeyed Abraham, calling him "lord."
You are her children when you do what is good
and fear no intimidation.

Likewise, you husbands should live with your wives in understanding,
showing honor to the weaker female sex,
since we are joint heirs of the gift of life,
so that your prayers may not be hindered.

Finally, all of you, be of one mind, sympathetic,
loving toward one another, compassionate, humble.

Do not return evil for evil, or insult for insult;
but, on the contrary, a blessing, because to this you were called,
that you might inherit a blessing.

The word of the Lord.

164.

12

1 John 3:18-24

A reading from the first Letter of Saint John

Love in deed and in truth.

Children, let us love not in word or speech
but in deed and truth.

Now this is how we shall know that we belong to the truth
and reassure our hearts before him
in whatever our hearts condemn,
for God is greater than our hearts and knows everything.
Beloved, if our hearts do not condemn us,
we have confidence in God
and receive from him whatever we ask,
because we keep his commandments and do what pleases him.
And his commandment is this:
we should believe in the name of his Son, Jesus Christ,
and love one another just as he commanded us.
Those who keep his commandments remain in him, and he in them,
and the way we know that he remains in us
is from the Spirit that he gave us.

The word of the Lord.

165.

13

1 John 4:7-12

A reading from the first Letter of Saint John

God is love.

Beloved, let us love one another,
because love is of God
everyone who loves is begotten by God and knows God.
Whoever is without love does not know God, for God is love.
In this way the love of God was revealed to us:
God sent his only-begotten Son into the world
so that we might have life through him.
In this is love:
not that we have loved God, but that he loved us
and sent his Son as expiation for our sins.
Beloved, if God so loved us,
we also must love one another.
No one has ever seen God.
Yet, if we love one another, God remains in us,
and his love is brought to perfection in us.

The word of the Lord.

166.

14

Revelation 19:1, 5-9a

A reading from the Book of Revelation

Blessed are those who have been called to the wedding feast of the Lamb.

I, John, heard what sounded like the loud voice
of a great multitude in heaven, saying:

"Alleluia!
Salvation, glory, and might belong to our God."

A voice coming from the throne said:

"Praise our God, all you his servants,
and you who revere him, small and great."

Then I heard something like the sound of a great multitude
or the sound of rushing water or mighty peals of thunder,
as they said:
"Alleluia!
The Lord has established his reign,
our God, the almighty.
Let us rejoice and be glad
and give him glory.
For the wedding day of the Lamb has come,
his bride has made herself ready.
She was allowed to wear
a bright, clean linen garment."
(The linen represents the righteous deeds of the holy ones.)

Then the angel said to me,
"Write this:
Blessed are those who have been called
to the wedding feast of the Lamb."

The word of the Lord.

Responsorial Psalms

(Lectionary for Mass, no. 803)

167.

1 Psalm 33:12 and 18, 20-21, 22

℟. (5b) The earth is full of the goodness of the Lord.

Blessed the nation whose God is the Lord,
the people he has chosen as his heritage.
Yes, the Lord's eyes are on those who fear him,
who hope in his merciful love.

℟. The earth is full of the goodness of the Lord.

Our soul is waiting for the Lord.
He is our help and our shield.
In him do our hearts find joy.
We trust in his holy name.

℟. The earth is full of the goodness of the Lord.

May your merciful love be upon us,
as we hope in you, O Lord.

℟. The earth is full of the goodness of the Lord.

168.

2

Psalm 34:2-3, 4-5, 6-7, 8-9

℟. (2a) I will bless the Lord at all times.

or:

℟. (9a) Taste and see the goodness of the Lord.

I will bless the LORD at all times,
praise of him is always in my mouth.
In the LORD my soul shall make its boast;
the humble shall hear and be glad.

℟. I will bless the Lord at all times.

or:

℟. Taste and see the goodness of the Lord.

Glorify the LORD with me;
together let us praise his name.
I sought the LORD, and he answered me;
from all my terrors he set me free.

℟. I will bless the Lord at all times.

or:

℟. Taste and see the goodness of the Lord.

Look toward him and be radiant;
let your faces not be abashed.
This lowly one called; the LORD heard,
and rescued him from all his distress.

℟. I will bless the Lord at all times.

or:

℟. Taste and see the goodness of the Lord.

The angel of the LORD is encamped
around those who fear him, to rescue them.
Taste and see that the LORD is good.
Blessed the man who seeks refuge in him.

℟. I will bless the Lord at all times.

or:

℟. Taste and see the goodness of the Lord.

169.

3

Psalm 103:1-2, 8 and 13, 17-18a

℟. (8a) The Lord is kind and merciful.

or:

℟. (cf. 17) The Lord's kindness is everlasting to those who fear him.

Bless the LORD, O my soul,
and all within me, his holy name.
Bless the LORD, O my soul,
and never forget all his benefits.

℟. The Lord is kind and merciful.

or:

℟. The Lord's kindness is everlasting to those who fear him.

The LORD is compassionate and gracious,
slow to anger and rich in mercy.
As a father has compassion on his children,
the LORD's compassion is on those who fear him.

℟. The Lord is kind and merciful.

or:

℟. The Lord's kindness is everlasting to those who fear him.

But the mercy of the LORD is everlasting
upon those who hold him in fear,
upon children's children his righteousness,
for those who keep his covenant.

℟. The Lord is kind and merciful.

or:

℟. The Lord's kindness is everlasting to those who fear him.

170.

4

Psalm 112:1bc-2, 3-4, 5-7a, 7bc-8, 9

℟. (cf. 1) Blessed the man who greatly delights in the Lord's commands.

or:

℟. Alleluia.

Blessed the man who fears the LORD,
who takes great delight in his commandments.
His descendants shall be powerful on earth;
the generation of the upright will be blest.

℟. Blessed the man who greatly delights in the Lord's commands.

or:

℟. Alleluia.

Riches and wealth are in his house;
his righteousness stands firm forever.
A light rises in the darkness for the upright;
he is generous, merciful, and righteous.

℟. Blessed the man who greatly delights in the Lord's commands.

or:

℟. Alleluia.

It goes well for the man who deals generously and lends,
who conducts his affairs with justice.
He will never be moved;
forever shall the righteous be remembered.
He has no fear of evil news.

℟. Blessed the man who greatly delights in the Lord's commands.

or:

℟. Alleluia.

With a firm heart, he trusts in the LORD.
With a steadfast heart he will not fear;
he will see the downfall of his foes.

℟. Blessed the man who greatly delights in the Lord's commands.

or:

℟. Alleluia.

Openhanded, he gives to the poor;
his righteousness stands firm forever.
His might shall be exalted in glory.

℟. Blessed the man who greatly delights in the Lord's commands.

or:

℟. Alleluia.

*171.

5 Psalm 128:1-2, 3, 4-5ac and 6a

℟. (cf. 1a) Blessed are those who fear the Lord.

or:

℟. (4) See how the Lord blesses those who fear him.

Blessed are all who fear the LORD,
and walk in his ways!
By the labor of your hands you shall eat.
You will be blessed and prosper.

℟. Blessed are those who fear the Lord.

or:

℟. See how the Lord blesses those who fear him.

Your wife like a fruitful vine
in the heart of your house;
your children like shoots of the olive
around your table.

℟. Blessed are those who fear the Lord.

or:

℟. See how the Lord blesses those who fear him.

Indeed thus shall be blessed
the man who fears the LORD.
May the LORD bless you from Zion
all the days of your life!
May you see your children's children.

℟. Blessed are those who fear the Lord.

or:

℟. See how the Lord blesses those who fear him.

172.

6 Psalm 145:8-9, 10 and 15, 17-18

℟. (9a) How good is the Lord to all.

The LORD is kind and full of compassion,
slow to anger, abounding in mercy.
How good is the LORD to all,
compassionate to all his creatures.

℟. How good is the Lord to all.

All your works shall thank you, O LORD,
and all your faithful ones bless you.
The eyes of all look to you,
and you give them their food in due season.

℟. How good is the Lord to all.

The LORD is righteous in all his ways,
and holy in all his deeds.
The LORD is close to all who call him,
who call on him in truth.

℟. How good is the Lord to all.

173.

7

Psalm 148:1-2, 3-4, 9-10, 11-13ab, 13c-14a

℟. (13a) Let all praise the name of the Lord.

or:

℟. Alleluia.

Praise the LORD from the heavens;
praise him in the heights.
Praise him, all his angels;
praise him, all his hosts.

℟. Let all praise the name of the Lord.

or:

℟. Alleluia.

Praise him, sun and moon;
praise him, all shining stars.
Praise him, highest heavens,
and the waters above the heavens.

℟. Let all praise the name of the Lord.

or:

℟. Alleluia.

Mountains and all hills,
fruit trees and all cedars,
beasts, both wild and tame,
creeping things and birds on the wing.

℟. Let all praise the name of the Lord.

or:

℟. Alleluia.

Kings of the earth and all peoples,
princes and all judges of the earth,
young men and maidens as well,
the old and the young together.
Let them praise the name of the LORD,
for his name alone is exalted.

℟. Let all praise the name of the Lord.

or:

℟. Alleluia.

His splendor above heaven and earth.
He exalts the strength of his people.

℟. Let all praise the name of the Lord.

or:

℟. Alleluia.

Alleluia Verses and Verses before the Gospel

(Lectionary for Mass, no. 804)

174.

1 1 John 4:7b

Everyone who loves is begotten of God and knows God.

175.

2 1 John 4:8b and 11

God is love.
Let us love one another, as God has loved us.

176.

3 1 John 4:12

If we love one another,
God remains in us
and his love is brought to perfection in us.

177.

4 1 John 4:16

Whoever remains in love,
remains in God and God in him.

Gospel Readings

(Lectionary for Mass, no. 805)

178.

1 Matthew 5:1-12a

✠ **A reading from the holy Gospel according to Matthew**

Rejoice and be glad, for your reward will be great in heaven.

**When Jesus saw the crowds, he went up the mountain,
and after he had sat down, his disciples came to him.
He began to teach them, saying:**

**"Blessed are the poor in spirit,
for theirs is the Kingdom of heaven.
Blessed are they who mourn,
for they will be comforted.
Blessed are the meek,
for they will inherit the land.
Blessed are they who hunger and thirst for righteousness,
for they will be satisfied.
Blessed are the merciful,
for they will be shown mercy.
Blessed are the clean of heart,
for they will see God.
Blessed are the peacemakers,
for they will be called children of God.
Blessed are they who are persecuted for the sake of righteousness,
for theirs is the Kingdom of heaven.
Blessed are you when they insult you and persecute you
and utter every kind of evil against you falsely because of me.
Rejoice and be glad,
for your reward will be great in heaven."**

The Gospel of the Lord.

179.

2 Matthew 5:13-16

✠ **A reading from the holy Gospel according to Matthew**

You are the light of the world.

Jesus said to his disciples:
"You are the salt of the earth.
But if salt loses its taste, with what can it be seasoned?
It is no longer good for anything
but to be thrown out and trampled underfoot.
You are the light of the world.
A city set on a mountain cannot be hidden.
Nor do they light a lamp and then put it under a bushel basket;
it is set on a lamp stand,
here it gives light to all in the house.
Just so, your light must shine before others,
that they may see your good deeds
and glorify your heavenly Father."

The Gospel of the Lord.

180.

3 Matthew 7:21, 24-29

LONG FORM

✠ **A reading from the holy Gospel according to Matthew**

A wise man built his house on rock.

Jesus said to his disciples:
"Not everyone who says to me, 'Lord, Lord,'
will enter the Kingdom of heaven,
but only the one who does the will of my Father in heaven.

"Everyone who listens to these words of mine and acts on them
will be like a wise man who built his house on rock.
The rain fell, the floods came,
and the winds blew and buffeted the house.
But it did not collapse; it had been set solidly on rock.
And everyone who listens to these words of mine
but does not act on them
will be like a fool who built his house on sand.
The rain fell, the floods came,
and the winds blew and buffeted the house.
And it collapsed and was completely ruined."

When Jesus finished these words,
the crowds were astonished at his teaching,
for he taught them as one having authority,
and not as their scribes.

The Gospel of the Lord.

OR

SHORT FORM Matthew 7:21, 24-25

✠ A reading from the holy Gospel according to Matthew

A wise man built his house on rock.

Jesus said to his disciples:
"Not everyone who says to me, 'Lord, Lord,'
will enter the Kingdom of heaven,
but only the one who does the will of my Father in heaven.

"Everyone who listens to these words of mine and acts on them
will be like a wise man who built his house on rock.

The rain fell, the floods came,
and the winds blew and buffeted the house.
But it did not collapse;
it had been set solidly on rock.

The Gospel of the Lord.

*181.

4

Matthew 19:3-6

✠ **A reading from the holy Gospel according to Matthew**

What God has united, man must not separate.

Some Pharisees approached Jesus, and tested him, saying,
"Is it lawful for a man to divorce his wife for any cause whatever?"
He said in reply, "Have you not read that from the beginning the Creator *made them male and female* and said,
For this reason a man shall leave his father and mother
and be joined to his wife, and the two shall become one flesh?
So they are no longer two, but one flesh.
Therefore, what God has joined together, man must not separate."

The Gospel of the Lord.

182.

5

Matthew 22:35-40

✠ **A reading from the holy Gospel according to Matthew**

This is the greatest and the first commandment.
The second is like it.

One of the Pharisees, a scholar of the law, tested Jesus by asking,
"Teacher, which commandment in the law is the greatest?"
He said to him,
"You shall love the Lord, your God,
with all your heart,
with all your soul,
and with all your mind.
This is the greatest and the first commandment.
The second is like it:
You shall love your neighbor as yourself.
The whole law and the prophets depend on these two commandments."

The Gospel of the Lord.

*183.

6

Mark 10:6-9

✠ **A reading from the holy Gospel according to Mark**

They are no longer two, but one flesh.

Jesus said:
"From the beginning of creation,
God made them male and female.
For this reason a man shall leave his father and mother
and be joined to his wife,
and the two shall become one flesh.
So they are no longer two but one flesh.
Therefore what God has joined together,
no human being must separate."

The Gospel of the Lord.

*184.

7

John 2:1-11

✠ **A reading from the holy Gospel according to John**

Jesus did this as the beginning of his signs in Cana in Galilee.

There was a wedding in Cana in Galilee,
and the mother of Jesus was there.
Jesus and his disciples were also invited to the wedding.
When the wine ran short,
the mother of Jesus said to him,
"They have no wine."
And Jesus said to her,
"Woman, how does your concern affect me?
My hour has not yet come."
His mother said to the servers,
"Do whatever he tells you."

Now there were six stone water jars there for Jewish ceremonial washings,
each holding twenty to thirty gallons.
Jesus told them,
"Fill the jars with water."
So they filled them to the brim.
Then he told them,
"Draw some out now and take it to the headwaiter."
So they took it.
And when the headwaiter tasted the water that had become wine,
without knowing where it came from
(although the servants who had drawn the water knew),
the headwaiter called the bridegroom and said to him,
"Everyone serves good wine first,
and then when people have drunk freely, an inferior one;
but you have kept the good wine until now."
Jesus did this as the beginning of his signs in Cana in Galilee
and so revealed his glory,
and his disciples began to believe in him.

The Gospel of the Lord.

185.

8

John 15:9-12

✠ **A reading from the holy Gospel according to John**

Remain in my love.

Jesus said to his disciples:
"As the Father loves me, so I also love you.
Remain in my love.
If you keep my commandments, you will remain in my love,
just as I have kept my Father's commandments
and remain in his love.

"I have told you this so that my joy might be in you
and your joy might be complete.
This is my commandment: love one another as I love you."

The Gospel of the Lord.

186.

9

John 15:12-16

✠ **A reading from the holy Gospel according to John**

This is my commandment: love one another.

Jesus said to his disciples:
"This is my commandment: love one another as I love you.
No one has greater love than this,
to lay down one's life for one's friends.
You are my friends if you do what I command you.
I no longer call you slaves,
because a slave does not know what his master is doing.

I have called you friends,
because I have told you everything I have heard from my Father.
It was not you who chose me, but I who chose you
and appointed you to go and bear fruit that will remain,
so that whatever you ask the Father in my name he may give you."

The Gospel of the Lord.

187.

10

John 17:20-26

LONG FORM

✠ **A reading from the holy Gospel according to John**

That they may be brought to perfection as one.

Jesus raised his eyes to heaven and said:
"I pray not only for my disciples,
but also for those who will believe in me through their word,
so that they may all be one,
as you, Father, are in me and I in you,
that they also may be in us,
that the world may believe that you sent me.
And I have given them the glory you gave me,
so that they may be one, as we are one,
I in them and you in me,
that they may be brought to perfection as one,
that the world may know that you sent me,
and that you loved them even as you loved me.
Father, they are your gift to me.

I wish that where I am they also may be with me,
that they may see my glory that you gave me,
because you loved me before the foundation of the world.
Righteous Father, the world also does not know you,
but I know you, and they know that you sent me.
I made known to them your name and I will make it known,
that the love with which you loved me
may be in them and I in them."

The Gospel of the Lord.

OR

SHORT FORM John 17:20-23

✠ **A reading from the holy Gospel according to John**

That they may be brought to perfection as one.

Jesus raised his eyes to heaven and said:
"Holy Father, I pray not only for these,
but also for those who will believe in me through their word,
so that they may all be one,
as you, Father, are in me and I in you,
that they also may be in us,
that the world may believe that you sent me.
And I have given them the glory you gave me,
so that they may be one, as we are one,
I in them and you in me,
that they may be brought to perfection as one,
that the world may know that you sent me,
and that you loved them even as you loved me."

The Gospel of the Lord.

II. COLLECTS

188. This Collect may not be used in the same celebration as the first Nuptial Blessing (nos. 74, 105).

1

O God, who consecrated the bond of Marriage
by so great a mystery
that in the wedding covenant you foreshadow
the Sacrament of Christ and his Church,
grant, we pray, to these your servants,
that what they receive in faith
they may live out in deeds.
Through our Lord Jesus Christ, your Son,
who lives and reigns with you
in the unity of the Holy Spirit,
one God, for ever and ever.

189.

2

O God, who in creating the human race
willed that man and wife should be one,
join, we pray, in a bond of inseparable love
these your servants who are to be united
in the covenant of Marriage,
so that, as you make their love fruitful,
they may become, by your grace,
witnesses to charity itself.
Through our Lord Jesus Christ, your Son,
who lives and reigns with you
in the unity of the Holy Spirit,
one God, for ever and ever.

190.

3

Be attentive to our prayers, O Lord,
and in your kindness
pour out your grace on these your servants (N. and N.),
that, coming together before your altar,
they may be confirmed in love for one another.
Through our Lord Jesus Christ, your Son,
who lives and reigns with you
in the unity of the Holy Spirit,
one God, for ever and ever.

191.

4

Grant, we pray, almighty God,
that these your servants,
now to be joined by the Sacrament of Matrimony,
may grow in the faith they profess
and enrich your Church with faithful offspring.
Through our Lord Jesus Christ, your Son,
who lives and reigns with you
in the unity of the Holy Spirit,
one God, for ever and ever.

192.

5

Be attentive to our prayers, O Lord,
and in your kindness uphold
what you have established
for the increase of the human race,
so that the union you have created
may be kept safe by your assistance.

Through our Lord Jesus Christ, your Son,
who lives and reigns with you
in the unity of the Holy Spirit,
one God, for ever and ever.

193.

6

O God, who since the beginning of the world
have blessed the increase of offspring,
show favor to our supplications
and pour forth the help of your blessing
on these your servants (N. and N.),
so that in the union of Marriage
they may be bound together
in mutual affection,
in likeness of mind,
and in shared holiness.
Through our Lord Jesus Christ, your Son,
who lives and reigns with you
in the unity of the Holy Spirit,
one God, for ever and ever.

III. OTHER PRAYERS FOR THE BLESSING OF RINGS

194.

1

Bless, O Lord, these rings,
which we bless ✠ in your name,
so that those who wear them
may remain entirely faithful to each other,
abide in peace and in your will,
and live always in mutual charity.
Through Christ our Lord.

195.

2

Bless ✠ and sanctify your servants
in their love, O Lord,
and let these rings, a sign of their faithfulness,
remind them of their love for one another.
Through Christ our Lord.

IV. PRAYERS OVER THE OFFERINGS

196.

1

Receive, we pray, O Lord,
the offering made on the occasion
of this sealing of the sacred bond of Marriage,
and, just as your goodness is its origin,
may your providence guide its course.
Through Christ our Lord.

197.

2

Receive in your kindness, Lord,
the offerings we bring in gladness before you,
and in your fatherly love
watch over those you have joined
in a sacramental covenant.
Through Christ our Lord.

198.

3

Show favor to our supplications, O Lord,
and receive with a kindly countenance
the oblations we offer for these your servants,
joined now in a holy covenant,
that through these mysteries
they may be strengthened
in love for one another and for you.
Through Christ our Lord.

V. PREFACES

199. The dignity of the Marriage covenant.

1

It is truly right and just, our duty and our salvation,
always and everywhere to give you thanks,
Lord, holy Father, almighty and eternal God.

For you have forged the covenant of Marriage
as a sweet yoke of harmony
and an unbreakable bond of peace,
so that the chaste and fruitful love of holy Matrimony
may serve to increase the children you adopt as your own.

By your providence and grace, O Lord,
you accomplish the wonder of this twofold design:
that, while the birth of children brings beauty to the world,
their rebirth in Baptism gives increase to the Church,
through Christ our Lord.

Through him, with the Angels and all the Saints,
we sing the hymn of your praise,
as without end we acclaim:

200. The great Sacrament of Matrimony.

2

It is truly right and just, our duty and our salvation,
always and everywhere to give you thanks,
Lord, holy Father, almighty and eternal God,
through Christ our Lord.

For in him you have made a new covenant
with your people,
so that, as you have redeemed man and woman
by the mystery of Christ's Death and Resurrection,
so in Christ you might make them
partakers of divine nature
and joint heirs with him of heavenly glory.

In the union of husband and wife
you give a sign of Christ's loving gift of grace,
so that the Sacrament we celebrate
might draw us back more deeply
into the wondrous design of your love.

And so, with the Angels and all the Saints,
we praise you, and without end we acclaim:

201. Matrimony as a sign of divine love.

3

**It is truly right and just, our duty and our salvation,
always and everywhere to give you thanks,
Lord, holy Father, almighty and eternal God.**

**For you willed that the human race,
created by the gift of your goodness,
should be raised to such high dignity
that in the union of husband and wife
you might bestow a true image of your love.**

**For those you created out of charity
you call to the law of charity without ceasing
and grant them a share in your eternal charity.**

**And so, the Sacrament of holy Matrimony,
as the abiding sign of your own love,
consecrates the love of man and woman,
through Christ our Lord.**

**Through him, with the Angels and all the Saints,
we sing the hymn of your praise,
as without end we acclaim:**

VI. COMMEMORATION OF THE COUPLE IN THE EUCHARISTIC PRAYER

a) In Eucharistic Prayer I

202. The proper form of the Hanc igitur (Therefore, Lord, we pray) is said. The words in parentheses may be omitted, if the occasion so suggests.

Therefore, Lord, we pray:
graciously accept this oblation of our service,
the offering of your servants N. and N.
and of your whole family,
who entreat your majesty on their behalf;
and as you have brought them to their wedding day,
so (gladden them with your gift
of the children they desire and)
bring them in your kindness
to the length of days for which they hope.
(Through Christ our Lord. Amen.)

b) In Eucharistic Prayer II

203. After the words and all the clergy, the following is added:

Be mindful also, Lord, of N. and N.,
whom you have brought to their wedding day,
so that by your grace
they may abide in mutual love and in peace.

c) In Eucharistic Prayer III

204. After the words **whom you have summoned before you**, the following is added:

Strengthen, we pray, in the grace of Marriage N. and N.,
whom you have brought happily to their wedding day,
that under your protection
they may always be faithful in their lives
to the covenant they have sealed in your presence.
In your compassion, O merciful Father,
gather to yourself all your children
scattered throughout the world.

VII. OTHER PRAYERS OF NUPTIAL BLESSING

205. In the invitation, if one or both of the spouses will not be receiving Communion, the words in parentheses are omitted. In the prayer, the words in parentheses may be omitted if it seems that circumstances suggest it, for example, if the bride and bridegroom are advanced in years.

205A. The Priest (or Deacon), with hands joined, calls upon those present to pray, saying:

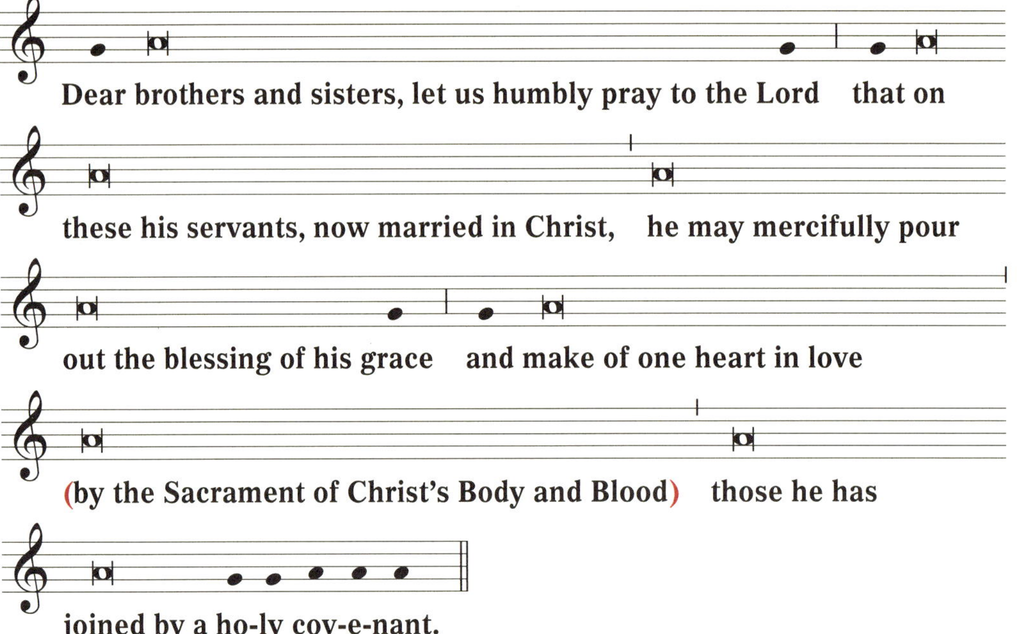

Dear brothers and sisters,
let us humbly pray to the Lord
that on these his servants, now married in Christ,
he may mercifully pour out
the blessing of his grace
and make of one heart in love
(by the Sacrament of Christ's Body and Blood)
those he has joined by a holy covenant.

Or:

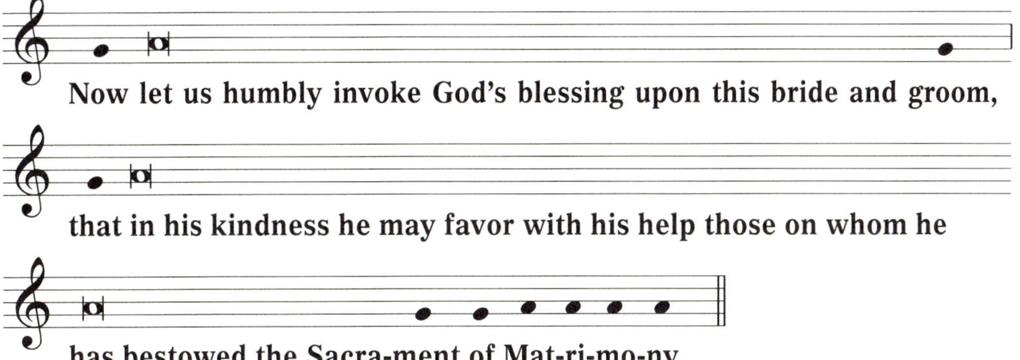

Now let us humbly invoke God's blessing
upon this bride and groom,
that in his kindness he may favor with his help
those on whom he has bestowed
the Sacrament of Matrimony.

And all pray in silence for a while.

205B. Then the Priest (or Deacon), with hands extended over the bride and bridegroom, continues:

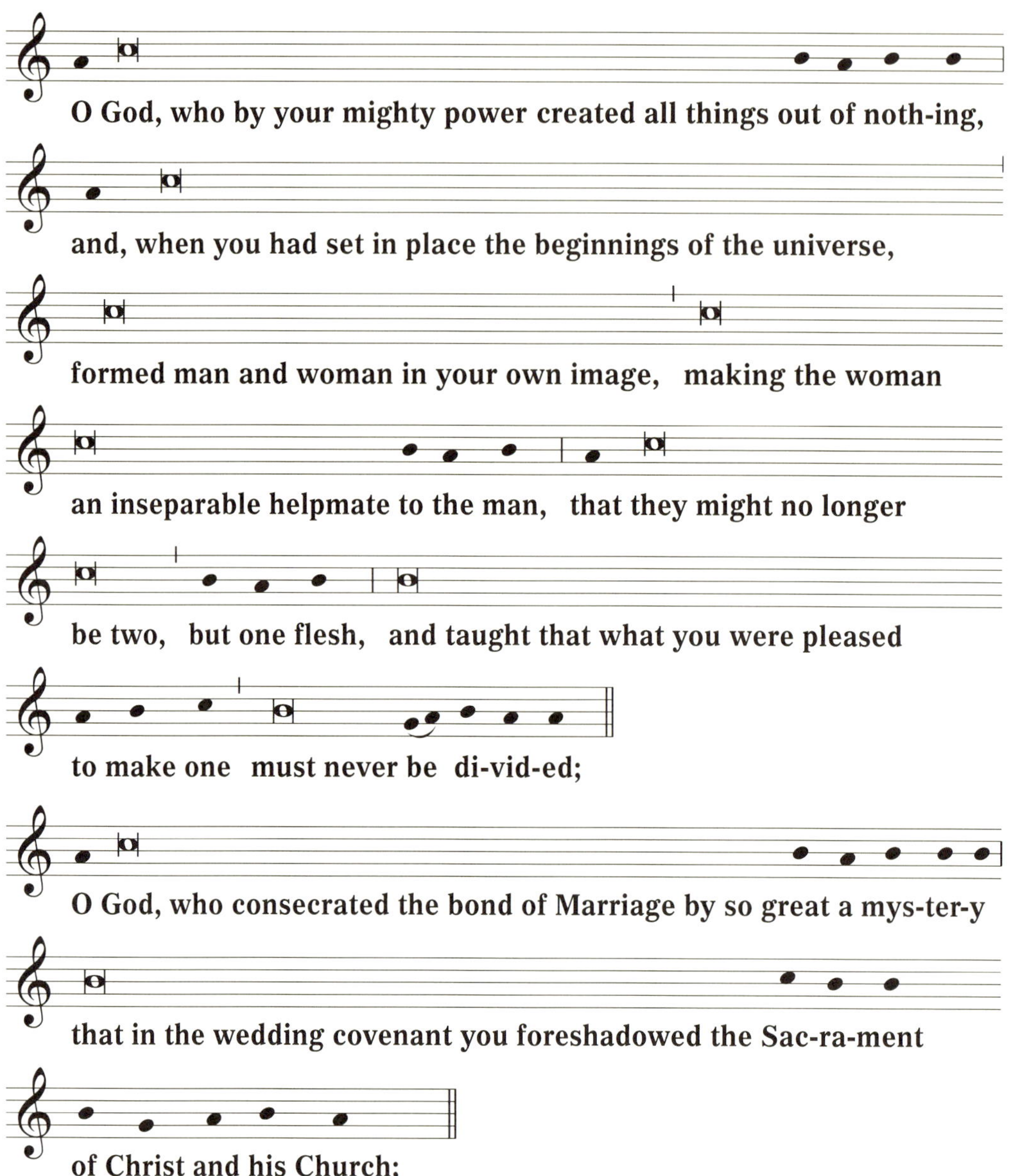
O God, who by your mighty power created all things out of noth-ing,
and, when you had set in place the beginnings of the universe,
formed man and woman in your own image, making the woman
an inseparable helpmate to the man, that they might no longer
be two, but one flesh, and taught that what you were pleased
to make one must never be di-vid-ed;
O God, who consecrated the bond of Marriage by so great a mys-ter-y
that in the wedding covenant you foreshadowed the Sac-ra-ment
of Christ and his Church;

O God, by whom woman is joined to man and the companionship
they had in the beginning is endowed with the one bless-ing
not forfeited by orig-i-nal sin nor washed a-way by the flood.
Look now with favor on these your ser-vants, joined together in
Mar-riage, who ask to be strengthened by your bless-ing. Send
down on them the grace of the Ho-ly Spir-it and pour your love
in-to their hearts, that they may remain faithful in the Mar-riage
cov-e-nant.
May the grace of love and peace abide in your daughter N.,
and let her always follow the example of those ho-ly wom-en
whose praises are sung in the Scrip-tures.

May her husband entrust his heart to her, so that, acknowledging
her as his equal and his joint heir to the life of grace, he may show
her due hon-or and cher-ish her al-ways with the love that Christ
has for his Church.
And now, Lord, we im-plore you: may these your servants hold fast
to the faith and keep your com-mand-ments; made one in the flesh,
may they be blame-less in all they do; and with the strength that
comes from the Gos-pel, may they bear true wit-ness to Christ
be-fore all; (may they be blessed with chil-dren, and prove
themselves virtuous par-ents, who live to see their chil-dren's
chil-dren).

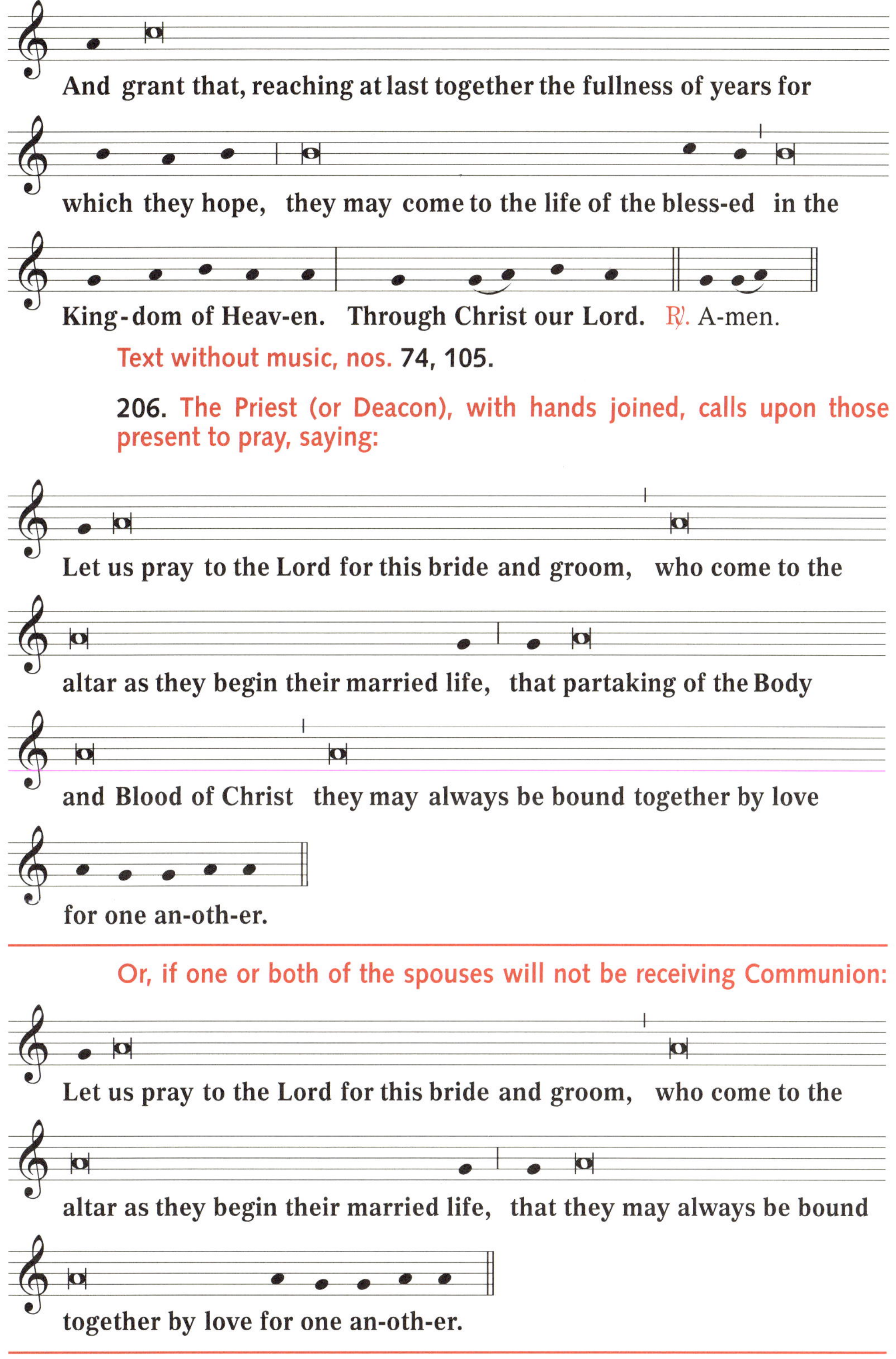

Text without music, nos. 74, 105.

206. The Priest (or Deacon), with hands joined, calls upon those present to pray, saying:

Or, if one or both of the spouses will not be receiving Communion:

Let us pray to the Lord for this bride and groom, who come to the altar as they begin their married life, that (partaking of the Body and Blood of Christ) they may always be bound together by love for one another.

And all pray in silence for a while.

207. Then the Priest (or Deacon), with hands extended over the bride and bridegroom, continues:

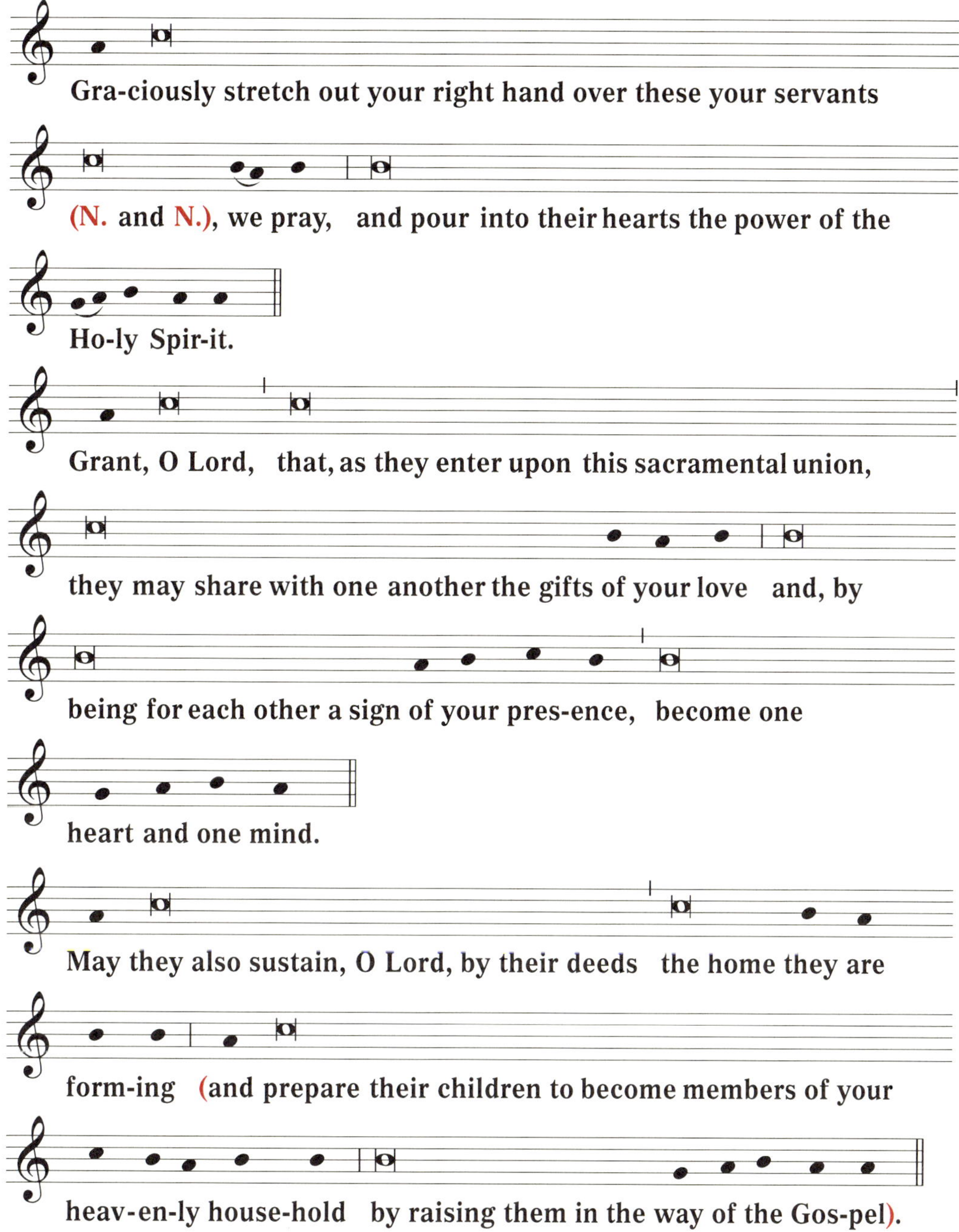
Gra-ciously stretch out your right hand over these your servants
(N. and N.), we pray, and pour into their hearts the power of the
Ho-ly Spir-it.
Grant, O Lord, that, as they enter upon this sacramental union,
they may share with one another the gifts of your love and, by
being for each other a sign of your pres-ence, become one
heart and one mind.
May they also sustain, O Lord, by their deeds the home they are
form-ing (and prepare their children to become members of your
heav-en-ly house-hold by raising them in the way of the Gos-pel).

Or, if the bride and bridegroom are advanced in years:

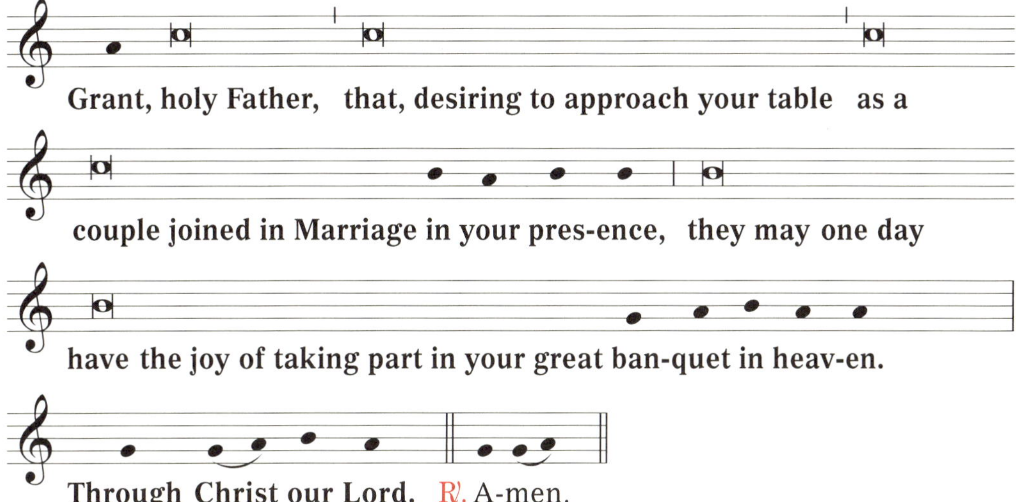

Text without music:

Holy Father,
who formed man in your own image,
male and female you created them,
so that as husband and wife, united in body and heart,
they might fulfill their calling in the world;

O God, who, to reveal the great design
you formed in your love,
willed that the love of spouses for each other
should foreshadow the covenant you graciously made
with your people,
so that, by fulfillment of the sacramental sign,
the mystical marriage of Christ with his Church
might become manifest
in the union of husband and wife among your faithful;

Graciously stretch out your right hand
over these your servants (N. and N.), we pray,
and pour into their hearts the power
of the Holy Spirit.

Grant, O Lord,
that, as they enter upon this sacramental union,
they may share with one another the gifts of your love
and, by being for each other a sign of your presence,
become one heart and one mind.

May they also sustain, O Lord, by their deeds
the home they are forming
(and prepare their children
to become members of your heavenly household
by raising them in the way of the Gospel).

Graciously crown with your blessings your daughter N.,
so that, by being a good wife (and mother),
she may bring warmth to her home
with a love that is pure
and adorn it with welcoming graciousness.

Bestow a heavenly blessing also, O Lord,
on N., your servant,
that he may be a worthy, good and
faithful husband (and a provident father).

Grant, holy Father,
that, desiring to approach your table
as a couple joined in Marriage in your presence,
they may one day have the joy
of taking part in your great banquet in heaven.
Through Christ our Lord.

℟. Amen.

208. The Priest (or Deacon), standing and turned toward the bride and bridegroom, with hands joined, calls upon those present to pray:

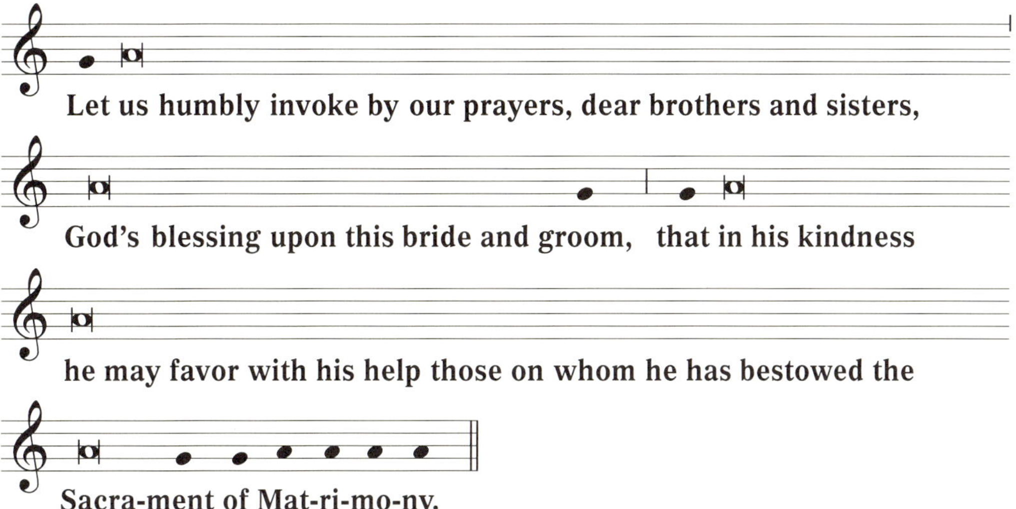

Let us humbly invoke by our prayers,
dear brothers and sisters,
God's blessing upon this bride and groom,
that in his kindness he may favor with his help
those on whom he has bestowed
the Sacrament of Matrimony.

And all pray in silence for a while.

209. Then the Priest (or Deacon), with hands extended over the bride and bridegroom, continues:

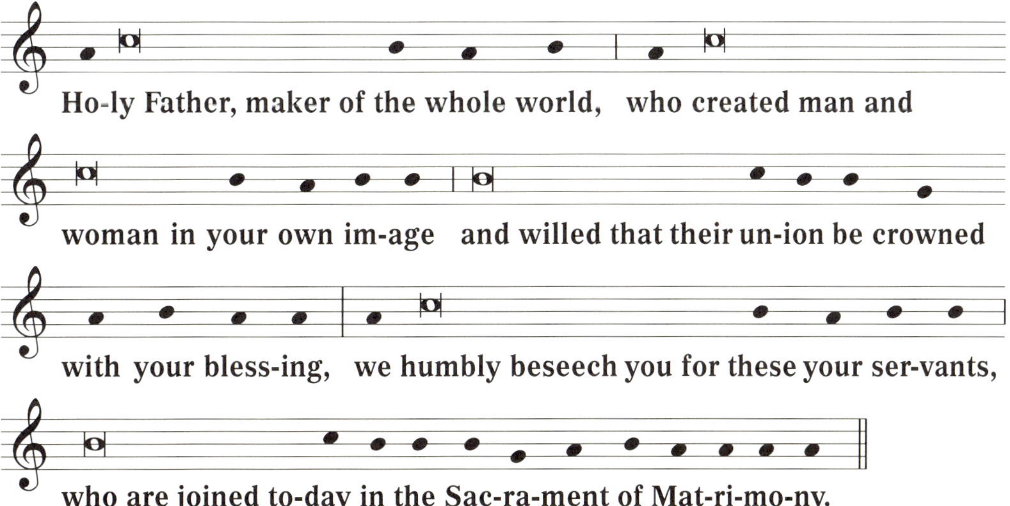

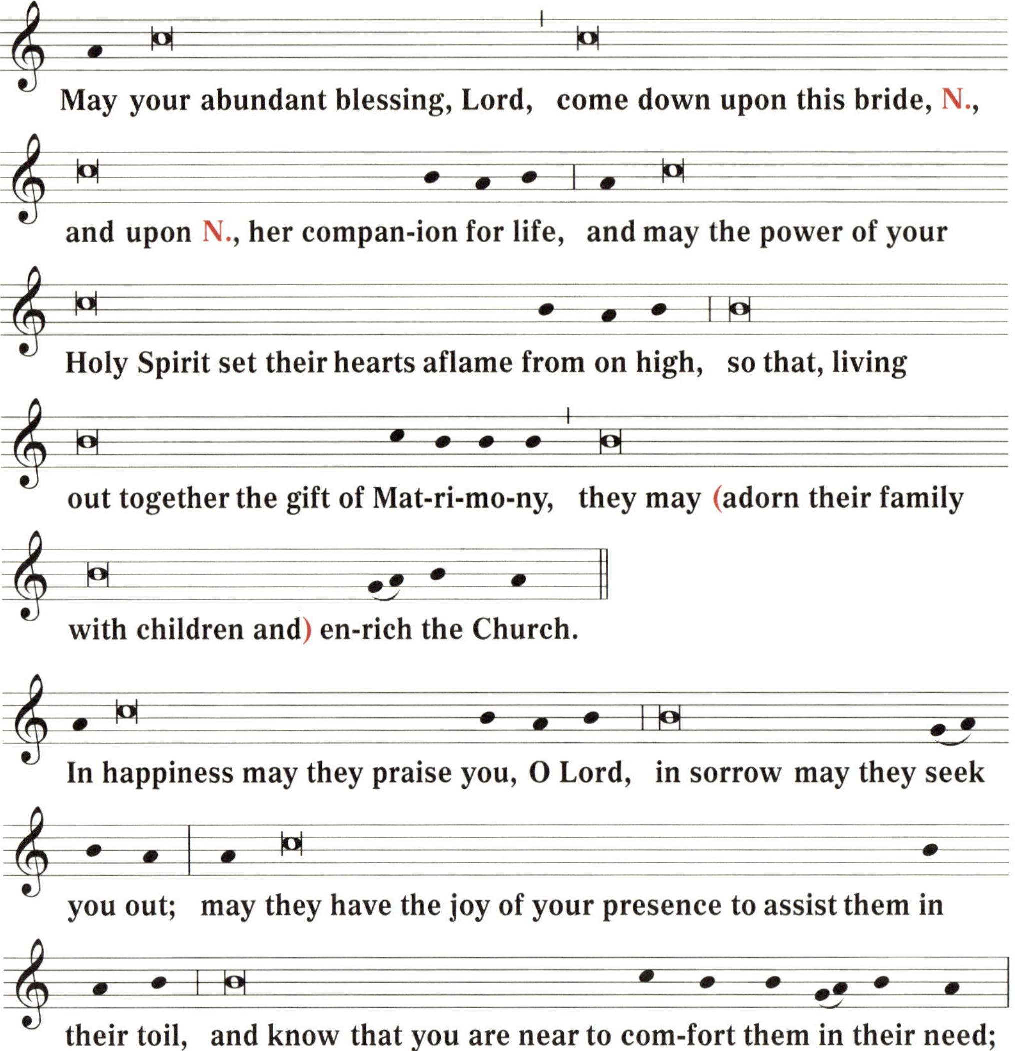
May your abundant blessing, Lord, come down upon this bride, N.,
and upon N., her compan-ion for life, and may the power of your
Holy Spirit set their hearts aflame from on high, so that, living
out together the gift of Mat-ri-mo-ny, they may (adorn their family
with children and) en-rich the Church.
In happiness may they praise you, O Lord, in sorrow may they seek
you out; may they have the joy of your presence to assist them in
their toil, and know that you are near to com-fort them in their need;

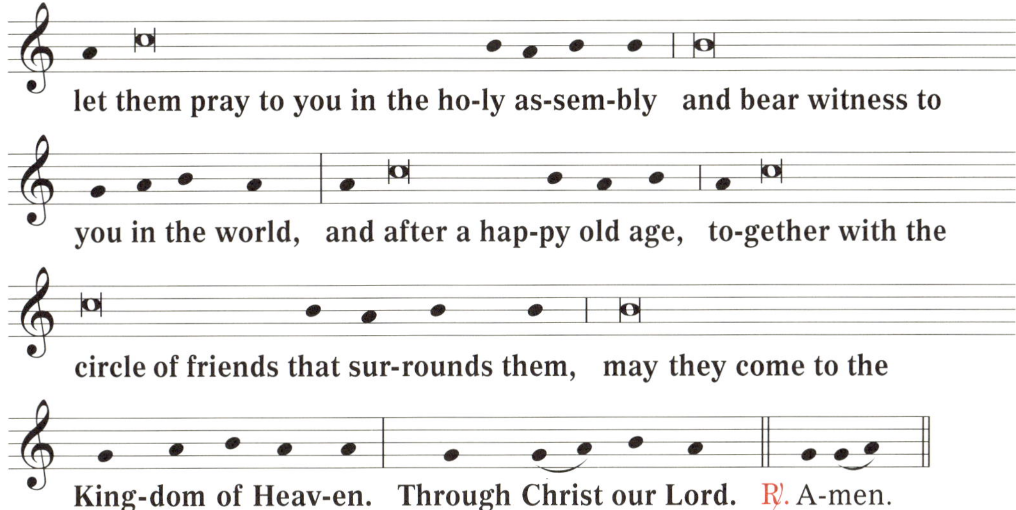

Text without music:

Holy Father, maker of the whole world,
who created man and woman in your own image
and willed that their union be crowned
with your blessing,
we humbly beseech you for these your servants,
who are joined today in the Sacrament of Matrimony.

May your abundant blessing, Lord,
come down upon this bride, N.,
and upon N., her companion for life,
and may the power of your Holy Spirit
set their hearts aflame from on high,
so that, living out together the gift of Matrimony,
they may (adorn their family with children
and) enrich the Church.

In happiness may they praise you, O Lord,
in sorrow may they seek you out;
may they have the joy of your presence
to assist them in their toil,
and know that you are near
to comfort them in their need;

**let them pray to you in the holy assembly
and bear witness to you in the world,
and after a happy old age,
together with the circle of friends
that surrounds them,
may they come to the Kingdom of Heaven.
Through Christ our Lord.**

℟. Amen.

VIII. PRAYERS AFTER COMMUNION

210.

1

**By the power of this sacrifice, O Lord,
accompany with your loving favor
what in your providence you have instituted,
so as to make of one heart in love
those you have already joined in this holy union
(and replenished with the one Bread
and the one Chalice).
Through Christ our Lord.**

211.

2

**Having been made partakers at your table,
we pray, O Lord,
that those who are united by the Sacrament of Marriage
may always hold fast to you
and proclaim your name to the world.
Through Christ our Lord.**

212.

3

**Grant, we pray, almighty God,
that the power of the Sacrament we have received
may find growth in these your servants**

and that the effects of the sacrifice we have offered
may be felt by us all.
Through Christ our Lord.

IX. BLESSINGS AT THE END OF THE CELEBRATION

213.

1

May God the eternal Father
keep you of one heart in love for one another,
that the peace of Christ may dwell in you
and abide always in your home.
℟. Amen.

May you be blessed in your children,
have solace in your friends
and enjoy true peace with everyone.
℟. Amen.

May you be witnesses in the world to God's charity,
so that the afflicted and needy
who have known your kindness
may one day receive you thankfully
into the eternal dwelling of God.
℟. Amen.

And may almighty God bless all of you,
who are gathered here,
the Father, and the Son, ✠ and the Holy Spirit.
℟. Amen.

214.

2

May God the all-powerful Father grant you his joy
and bless you in your children.
℟. Amen.

May the Only Begotten Son of God
stand by you with compassion in good times
and in bad.
℟. Amen.

May the Holy Spirit of God
always pour forth his love into your hearts.
℟. Amen.

And may almighty God bless all of you,
who are gathered here,
the Father, and the Son, ✠ and the Holy Spirit.
℟. Amen.

215.

3

May the Lord Jesus,
who graced the marriage at Cana by his presence,
bless you and your loved ones.
℟. Amen.

May he, who loved the Church to the end,
unceasingly pour his love into your hearts.
℟. Amen.

May the Lord grant
that, bearing witness to faith in his Resurrection,
you may await with joy the blessed hope to come.
℟. Amen.

And may almighty God bless all of you,
who are gathered here,
the Father, and the Son, ✠ and the Holy Spirit.
℟. Amen.

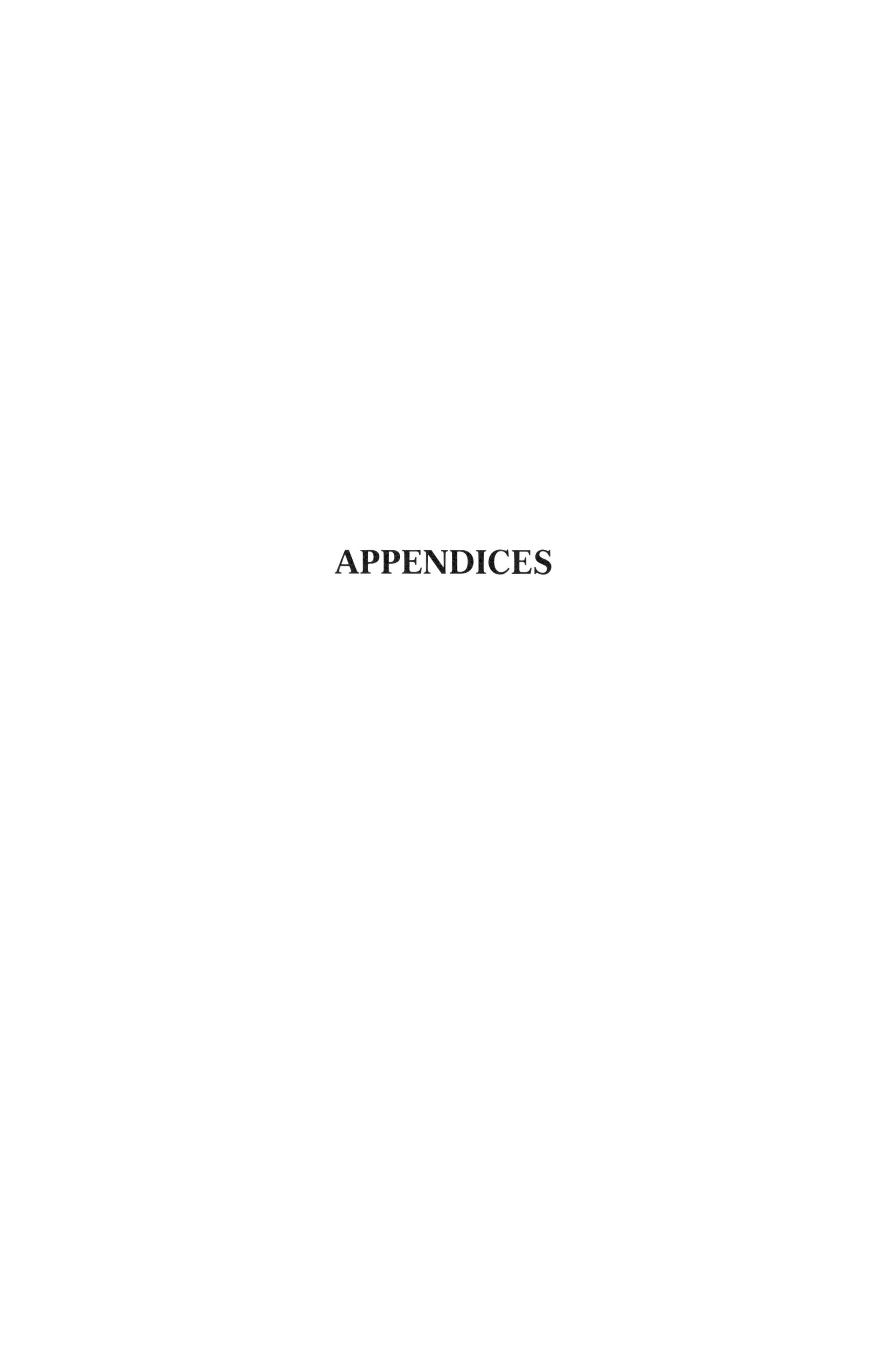

APPENDICES

I. EXAMPLES OF THE UNIVERSAL PRAYER

216.

1

**Dear brothers and sisters,
as we call to mind the special gift of grace and charity
by which God has been pleased to crown and consecrate
the love of our sister N. and our brother N.,
let us commend them to the Lord.**

**That these faithful Christians, N. and N.,
newly joined in Holy Matrimony,
may always enjoy health and well-being,
let us pray to the Lord.**

℟. Lord, we ask you, hear our prayer.

Or another appropriate response of the people.

**That he will bless their covenant
as he chose to sanctify marriage at Cana in Galilee,
let us pray to the Lord.**

℟. Lord, we ask you, hear our prayer.

**That they be granted perfect and fruitful love,
peace and strength,
and that they bear faithful witness
to the name of Christian,
let us pray to the Lord.**

℟. Lord, we ask you, hear our prayer.

**That the Christian people
may grow in virtue day by day
and that all who are burdened by any need
may receive the help of grace from above,
let us pray to the Lord.**

℟. Lord, we ask you, hear our prayer.

That the grace of the Sacrament
will be renewed by the Holy Spirit
in all married persons here present,
let us pray to the Lord.

℟. Lord, we ask you, hear our prayer.

Graciously pour out upon this husband and wife,
O Lord,
the Spirit of your love,
to make them one heart and one soul,
so that nothing whatever may divide
those you have joined
and no harm come to those you have filled with your blessing.
Through Christ our Lord.

℟. Amen.

217.

2

Dear brothers and sisters,
let us accompany this new family with our prayers,
that the mutual love of this couple may grow daily
and that God in his kindness
will sustain all families throughout the world.

For this bride and groom,
and for their well-being as a family,
let us pray to the Lord.

℟. Lord, we ask you, hear our prayer.

Or another appropriate response of the people.

For their relatives and friends,
and for all who have assisted this couple,
let us pray to the Lord.

℟. Lord, we ask you, hear our prayer.

For young people preparing to enter Marriage,
and for all whom the Lord is calling
to another state in life,
let us pray to the Lord.

℟. Lord, we ask you, hear our prayer.

For all families throughout the world
and for lasting peace among all people,
let us pray to the Lord.

℟. Lord, we ask you, hear our prayer.

For all members of our families
who have passed from this world,
and for all the departed,
let us pray to the Lord.

℟. Lord, we ask you, hear our prayer.

For the Church, the holy People of God,
and for unity among all Christians,
let us pray to the Lord.

℟. Lord, we ask you, hear our prayer.

Lord Jesus, who are present in our midst,
as N. and N. seal their union
accept our prayer
and fill us with your Spirit.
Who live and reign for ever and ever.

℟. Amen.

II. THE ORDER OF BLESSING AN ENGAGED COUPLE

INTRODUCTION

218. Among the responsibilities of Christian spouses and the ways in which their apostolate is exercised, in addition to the upbringing of children, the assistance offered to engaged couples, so that they may better prepare themselves for Marriage, is clearly of considerable importance.

The honorable betrothal of Christians, therefore, is a special occasion for two families, appropriately celebrated with some ceremony and with common prayer, so that, upon receiving the divine blessing, what is joyfully begun may in its own time be joyfully completed.

This celebration must be adapted to suit particular circumstances.

219. When the engagement is celebrated within the confines of the two families, one of the parents may appropriately preside at the rite of blessing. If a Priest or a Deacon is present, however, then the office of presiding more appropriately belongs to him, provided that it is clear to those present that the rite is not a celebration of Marriage itself.

220. The order supplied here, therefore, may be used either by the parents, or by a Priest, a Deacon, or another layperson, who, while maintaining the chief elements and structure of the rite, should adapt the individual parts to the circumstances.

221. If the engagement has already taken place, this order of celebration may also be used when couples are brought together for catechetical preparation for Marriage. A betrothal or a special blessing of an engaged couple, however, is never to be combined with the celebration of Mass.

The Introductory Rites

222. When the families are gathered, if a Priest or a Deacon presides, after the Sign of the Cross has been made, he greets those present, saying:

Grace to you and peace
from our Lord Jesus Christ,
who loved us and gave himself up for us.

Or other suitable words, especially words taken from *The Roman Missal.*

All reply:

And with your spirit.

---

223. If the minister is a layperson, after the Sign of the Cross has been made, he or she greets those present, saying:

Brothers and sisters,
let us praise our Lord Jesus Christ,
who loved us and gave himself up for us.

All reply:

Amen.

---

224. Then, in these or similar words, the minister disposes those present for reception of the blessing:

We know that God's grace is a constant need
for everyone, at all times.
Yet no one can doubt
that members of Christ's faithful have
special need of that grace
when they are preparing to form a new family.
And so, let us ask God's blessing
upon our brother and sister (N. and N.),
that they may grow in mutual respect,
love each other more deeply,
and approach the celebration of holy Matrimony chastely
through appropriate companionship and prayer together.

Reading of the Word of God

225. Then, one of those present or the minister reads a text of Sacred Scripture.

John 15:9-12

**Listen, brothers and sisters,
to the words of the holy Gospel according to John.**

This is my commandment: love one another as I love you.

**Jesus said to his disciples:
"As the Father loves me, so I also love you.
Remain in my love.
If you keep my commandments, you will remain in my love,
just as I have kept my Father's commandments
and remain in his love.**

**"I have told you this so that my joy might be in you
and your joy might be complete.
This is my commandment: love one another as I love you."**

The Gospel of the Lord.

℟. Praise to you, Lord Jesus Christ.

226. Or:

1 Corinthians 13:4-13

Listen, brothers and sisters,
to the words of the Apostle Paul to the Corinthians.

Love believes all things, hopes all things, endures all things.

Love is patient, love is kind.
It is not jealous, it is not pompous,
it is not inflated, it is not rude,
it does not seek its own interests,
it is not quick-tempered, it does not brood over injury,
it does not rejoice over wrongdoing
but rejoices with the truth.
It bears all things, believes all things,
hopes all things, endures all things.
Love never fails.
If there are prophecies, they will be brought to nothing;
if tongues, they will cease;
if knowledge, it will be brought to nothing.
For we know partially and we prophesy partially,
but when the perfect comes, the partial will pass away.
When I was a child, I used to talk as a child,
think as a child, reason as a child;
when I became a man, I put aside childish things.
At present we see indistinctly, as in a mirror,
but then face to face.
At present I know partially;
then I shall know fully, as I am fully known.
So faith, hope, love remain, these three;
but the greatest of these is love.

The word of the Lord.

℟. Thanks be to God.

227. Or:

Hosea 2:21-26

**Listen, brothers and sisters,
to the words of the Prophet Hosea.**

I will espouse you to me in fidelity.

**Thus says the Lord to Zion:
I will espouse you to me forever:
I will espouse you in right and in justice,
in love and mercy;
I will espouse you in fidelity,
and you shall know the Lord.**

**On that day I will respond, says the Lord;
I will respond to the heavens,
and they shall respond to the earth;
The earth shall respond to the grain, and wine, and oil,
and these shall respond to Jezreel.
I will sow him for myself in the land,
and I will have pity on Lo-ruhama.
I will say to Lo-ammi, "You are my people,"
and he shall say, "My God!"**

The word of the Lord.

℟. Thanks be to God.

Philippians 2:1-5

Listen, brothers and sisters,
to the words of the Apostle Paul to the Philippians.

Be of the same mind.

Brothers and sisters:
If there is any encouragement in Christ,
any solace in love,
any participation in the Spirit,
any compassion and mercy,
complete my joy by being of the same mind, with the same love,
united in heart, thinking one thing.
Do nothing out of selfishness or out of vainglory;
rather, humbly regard others as more important than yourselves,
each looking out not for his own interests,
but also for those of others.
Have in you the same attitude
that is also in Christ Jesus.

The word of the Lord.

℟. Thanks be to God.

228. If appropriate, there may be said or sung the following Responsorial Psalm or another suitable liturgical song.

Psalm 145:8-9, 10 and 15, 17-18

℟. (9a) How good is the Lord to all.

The Lord is kind and full of compassion,
slow to anger and abounding in mercy.
How good is the Lord to all,
compassionate to all his creatures.

℟. How good is the Lord to all.

All your works shall thank you, O LORD,
and all your faithful ones bless you.
The eyes of all look to you,
and you give them their food in due season.

℟. How good is the Lord to all.

The LORD is righteous in all his ways,
and holy in all his deeds.
The LORD is close to all who call him,
who call on him in truth.

℟. How good is the Lord to all.

229. The one who presides may briefly address those present, shedding light on the biblical reading, so that they may understand with faith the meaning of the celebration and may be able to distinguish it correctly from the celebration of Marriage.

PRAYERS

230. The common prayer follows. From the intercessions provided below, the one who presides may select those that seem more suitable or may add others that apply to particular circumstances:

With confidence, let us call on God the Father,
who so loved all people
that he made them his children in Christ
and revealed them to the world as witnesses of his love.

℟. Keep us in your love for ever, Lord.

Or another suitable response of the people.

You willed that mutual love
should make the brothers and sisters of Christ
known as your true children:

℟. Keep us in your love for ever, Lord.

You place upon men and women
the gentle demands of your love,
so that they may find happiness in accepting them:

℟. Keep us in your love for ever, Lord.

You bring a man and a woman together
in mutual delight,
that the family thus formed
may joyfully be crowned with children:

℟. Keep us in your love for ever, Lord.

Through Christ's paschal sacrifice,
by which he loved the Church
and presented her to you washed clean in his Blood
you mystically foreshadowed the fullness of wedded love
in the Sacrament of Matrimony:

℟. Keep us in your love for ever, Lord.

You call N. and N. to a full communion of love,
so that they may become one in mind and heart
as members of the Christian family:

℟. Keep us in your love for ever, Lord.

231. In accord with local custom, before the prayer of blessing, the engaged couple may express some sign of their promise to each other, for example, by signing a document or by the giving of rings or other gifts.

232. The engagement rings or gifts may be blessed with the following formula:

Safeguard the gifts you have exchanged,
so that you may fulfill in due time
the pledge you have offered each other.

℟. Amen.

Prayer of Blessing

233. Then the one who presides says the prayer with hands joined; if, however, he is a Priest or Deacon, he says the prayer with hands extended:

We give you praise, O Lord,
who in your gentle wisdom call and prepare
your son and daughter N. and N.
to love each other.

Graciously strengthen their hearts, we pray,
so that, by keeping faith and pleasing you in all things,
they may come happily to the Sacrament of Marriage.
Through Christ our Lord.

℟. Amen.

234. Or, when a Priest or Deacon presides:

Lord God, wellspring of all love,
N. and N. have met each other
through your providential plan.
Mercifully grant as they seek your grace
in preparing for the Sacrament of Marriage,
that, sustained by heavenly ✠ blessing,
they may grow in mutual respect
and may love each other with true charity.
Through Christ our Lord.

℟. Amen.

Conclusion of the Rite

235. Then, the one who presides concludes the rite, saying:

May the God of love and peace
dwell within you,
direct your steps,
and strengthen your hearts in his love.

All:

Amen.

236. It is a praiseworthy practice to end the celebration with a suitable chant.

III. THE ORDER OF BLESSING A MARRIED COUPLE WITHIN MASS ON THE ANNIVERSARY OF MARRIAGE

237. On the main anniversaries of Marriage, as for example, on the twenty-fifth, fiftieth, or sixtieth anniversary, it is fitting to hold a special remembrance of the Sacrament by means of the celebration of the proper Mass with the prayers indicated in *The Roman Missal* (Masses and Prayers for Various Needs and Occasions, 11. On the Anniversaries of Marriage).

238. In the Liturgy of the Word, the readings may be taken either from the Lectionary for the Celebration of Marriage (see above, nos. 144-187), or from the Mass for Giving Thanks to God from the Lectionary for Masses for Various Needs (cf. *The Roman Missal, Lectionary for Mass*, nos. 943-947) in accord with the norm of the rubrics.

239. After the reading of the Gospel, in a homily based on the sacred text, the Priest should expound the mystery and the grace of Christian married life, keeping in mind, however, the various circumstances of individuals.

240. Then, in these or similar words, the Priest invites the couple to pray in silence and to renew before God their commitment to live their Marriage in holiness.

N. and N.,
on the anniversary of that celebration
at which you joined your lives in an unbreakable bond
through the Sacrament of Matrimony,
you now intend to renew before the Lord
the promises you made to one another.
Turn to the Lord in prayer,
that these vows may be strengthened by divine grace.

241. Then the couple renew their commitment quietly.

242. If, however, the couple, taking circumstances into account, wish to renew their commitment publicly, the form provided here is used:

The husband:

Blessed are you, Lord,
for by your goodness I took N. as my wife.

The wife:

Blessed are you, Lord,
for by your goodness I took N. as my husband.

Both:

Blessed are you, Lord,
for in the good and the bad times of our life
you have stood lovingly by our side.
Help us, we pray,
to remain faithful in our love for one another,
so that we may be true witnesses
to the covenant you have made with humankind.

The Priest:

**May the Lord keep you safe all the days of your life.
May he be your comfort in adversity
and your support in prosperity.
May he fill your home with his blessings.
Through Christ our Lord.**

℟. Amen.

The Blessing of Rings

243. Then the Priest, if appropriate, says this prayer:

**Increase and sanctify, Lord,
the love of your servants N. and N.,
who once gave each other these rings
as a sign of faithfulness,
that they may always grow in the grace of the Sacrament.
Through Christ our Lord.**

℟. Amen.

And the rings may be honored with an incensation.

244. If, however, new rings are presented, the Priest says this prayer of blessing:

Bless and sanctify
the love of your servants, O Lord;
let these rings, a sign of their faithfulness,
remind them of their love for one another
and recall the grace of the Sacrament.
Through Christ our Lord.

℟. Amen.

Another formula, no. 194.

245. Then follows the Universal Prayer or Prayer of the Faithful in the form usual at Mass, or prayer in common in the form provided here:

Let us call upon the mercy of God the almighty Father,
who in his most provident plan
willed that the history of salvation
be signified in marital love and fidelity.
(marital love, fidelity and fruitfulness.)

℟. Renew the fidelity of your servants, Lord.

Holy Father, who are called faithful,
requiring and rewarding the observance of your covenant,
be pleased to fill with your blessings these your servants
who celebrate the (twenty-fifth, fiftieth, sixtieth) anniversary
of their Marriage.

℟. Renew the fidelity of your servants, Lord.

Holy Father, who with the Son and the Holy Spirit
enjoy from eternity
perfect oneness of life and communion of love,
grant that these your servants
may always remember and faithfully keep
the covenant of love they made in the Sacrament.

℟. Renew the fidelity of your servants, Lord.

Holy Father, who in your providence
order all the experiences of human life
so as to lead the faithful to share in the mystery of Christ,
grant that these your servants,
serenely accepting both good times and bad,
may strive to cling to Christ and live for him alone.

℟. Renew the fidelity of your servants, Lord.

Holy Father, who willed that the partnership
of Marriage
should be an example of Christian living,
grant that all married couples
may be witnesses in the world
to the mystery of your Son's love.

℟. Renew the fidelity of your servants, Lord.

246. The Priest concludes the prayer:

O God, in whose plan
family life has its firm foundation,
hear with compassion the prayers of your servants
and grant that,
following the example of the Holy Family,
they may praise you without end
in the joy of your house.
Through Christ our Lord.

℟. Amen.

247. In the Liturgy of the Eucharist everything takes place according to the Order of Mass, except what follows.

If appropriate, at the Presentation of the Gifts the husband and wife may bring the bread, wine, and water to the altar.

248. After the Our Father, the prayer Deliver us is omitted. The Priest, facing the couple, with hands extended, says:

We praise you, O God,
we bless you, Creator of all things,
who in the beginning made man and woman
that they might form a communion of life and love.
We also give you thanks
for graciously blessing the family life
of your servants N. and N.,
so that it might present an image of Christ's union with the Church.
Therefore look with kindness upon them today,
and as you have sustained their communion
amid joys and struggles,
renew their Marriage covenant each day,
increase their charity,
and strengthen in them the bond of peace,
so that (, together with the circle of their children that surrounds them,)
they may for ever enjoy your blessing.
Through Christ our Lord.

All reply:

Amen.

249. After The peace of the Lord has been said, if appropriate, in accordance with local customs, the couple and all others offer one another a sign that suitably expresses peace and charity.

250. The couple may receive Communion under both kinds.

251. At the end of Mass, the Priest blesses the couple and those present either in the usual manner or with a more solemn formula, for example, in the following way:

The Deacon invites those present to receive the blessing:

Bow down for the blessing.

Then the Priest, with hands extended over the couple, says:

May God the all-powerful Father
grant you his joy.

℟. Amen.

May the Only Begotten Son of God
stand by you with compassion in good times and in bad.

℟. Amen.

May the Holy Spirit
always pour forth his love into your hearts.

℟. Amen.

Finally, he blesses all present, adding:

And may almighty God bless all of you,
who are gathered here,
the Father, and the Son, ✠ and the Holy Spirit.

℟. Amen.